Understanding Momentum in Investment Technical Analysis

Understanding Momentum in Investment Technical Analysis

Making Better Predictions Based on Price, Trend Strength, and Speed of Change

Michael C. Thomsett

BEP BUSINESS EXPERT PRESS

Understanding Momentum in Investment Technical Analysis: Making Better Predictions Based on Price, Trend Strength, and Speed of Change

First published in 2019 by
Business Expert Press, LLC
222 East 46th Street, New York, NY 10017
www.businessexpertpress.com

ISBN-13: 978-1-94999-162-8 (paperback)
ISBN-13: 978-1-94999-163-5 (e-book)

Business Expert Press Finance and Financial Management Collection

Collection ISSN: 2331-0049 (print)
Collection ISSN: 2331-0057 (electronic)

Cover and interior design by Exeter Premedia Services Private Ltd., Chennai, India

First edition: 2019

10 9 8 7 6 5 4 3 2 1

Printed in the United States of America.

Abstract

The concept of momentum in chart analysis is of great interest to technical analysts. Momentum indicates the strength and speed of price movement, but not the direction. It enables, through the use of index calculations, identification of conditions when a stock's price is either overbought or oversold. Momentum is most effective when used as a confirming indicator for other signals found in price, volume, or moving averages. Often overlooked by traders focused on price reversals or continuation signals, momentum provides a context to price behavior and to the price trend.

Keywords

Overbought; oversold; moving average; oscillator; relative strength index; stochastic oscillator; rate of change; Bollinger Bands; reversal; confirmation

Contents

Introduction

The Nature of Momentum

Traders rely on an array of different signals, and among these are momentum oscillators. However, even while knowing *what* an oscillator is and what it shows, you might not necessarily know how to use an oscillator to time trades. This requires identification of turning points, confirmation, and determining the strength of price movement.

Momentum oscillators are measurements of the rate and strength of change in price, but not the direction of price movement. This points to a feature of momentum that some traders overlook: As a current trend accelerates, so does momentum (as measured by the oscillator). As the trend begins to weaken, it is often first seen in a slowing of momentum. In this regard, momentum often acts as a leading indicator, predicting what is going to change and what will be reflected in price later.

An initial assumption is that you understand the science of chart reading and know what momentum oscillators look like. For anyone not familiar with the stock chart, some basics must be mastered as a first step. These basics include the following:

1. *Charts are scaled based on price range.* The scaling of a chart might be very small, only fractions of a point. Or it could be large, with 10-point of 20-point spacing between points. It all depends on the price range for the period covered. This can be deceptive. A low-scaled chart might appear highly volatile even when only a few points of change have transpired. A high-scaled chart might appear to have low volatility even though dozens of points have been involved in the movement of price. Complicating matters, chart scaling might be adjusted so that the lower side is wider than the higher side. This occurs to fit all the trading activity into the fixed size of the chart.

2. *The attributes of a chart are relative.* Because scaling is dissimilar between two or more stock charts, it is not accurate to look at charts side by side and make judgments concerning price movement, volatility, or even the importance of gaps. Scaling makes chart reading inexact, and a wise analyst will be aware of this. The proper comparison is between current and past price behaviors, and not between two or more different charts.

3. *Comparisons are not reliable without signals.* A comparison between current and past price behaviors is not reliable as a method for timing trades. A popular criticism of technical analysis is that it cannot point to future price movement. This criticism assumes that technical traders rely on past price activity to predict the future, but this is not always the case. An informed technical trader understands that price behavior is only one aspect of timing trades. Beyond this, signals are essential. These include reversal or continuation signals, each with confirmation—both identified before making trades. Signals come in many forms: price, volume, moving averages, and momentum oscillators. The last form—oscillators—may work as a leading indicator, often found immediately before price reversals.

4. *There is no magic.* Some promoters of technical analysis promise that secret or magic signals point the way to fast and easy riches. This is never true. Chart reading is work, and the informed technical trader must be objective and able to act as a contrarian. This is the only method for beating the averages and correctly interpreting charts. A contrarian may be misunderstood as someone who always makes decisions against the market. In fact, the real distinction is that contrarians trade based on cold logic and analysis. In comparison, most traders are emotional. They trade out of greed as prices rise, and out of panic as prices fall. This explains why most traders time trades poorly and accumulate more losses than profits.

How do you acquire skills as a chart reader and trader? The answer lies in being able to distinguish strong signals from weak signals and in understanding the differences between momentum and other forms of indicator. Some experts mix in other types of signals, such as volume-based indicators, and call these "oscillators," but this book makes a clear distinction. Oscillators specifically relate to the speed and strength of trends. A volume signal is not an oscillator. It is one of many types of signals accompanying and confirming price indicators and trends and can be used in conjunction with oscillators to identify when a current trend is changing. The oscillator is distinctly different because it points to likely reversal or continuation based on the most recent price behavior; at the same time, finding momentum does not offer any assurance about future price levels. It only offers judgment about the character of a trend.

Oscillators, because they are based on the averages of price and volume, are thought of as lagging indicators. If this were true, they would be of little value in the timing of trade decisions based on slowing down of trends. However, despite the features that lag behind price, the changes in price movement witnessed in the oscillator also function as leading indicators. This is especially true in exceptionally volatile times, when price is continually moving outside of its normal and recently established trading range, only to retreat into range over and over. In such times of high volatility, you are likely to witness volume spikes and false signals in price. However, the momentum oscillator may be the most reliable indicator of whether the current trend is likely to continue or reverse.

This book focuses on the attributes of oscillators, not to provide basic information about trends and the analysis of direction, but to reveal ideas for the use of oscillators for trade timing. It is divided into three parts. Part I explains how the theory of "overbought" and "oversold" is applied in the study and analysis of price (and thus, in timing of coming reversal). In this section, moving averages are also examined in the way they work with momentum to anticipate changes in price trends.

Part II introduces five momentum indicators and explores what the calculation of each reveals. As with the first section, this is not an introductory discussion of signals, but a study of how they provide actionable trade timing.

Part III is a discussion of trading with oscillators. This includes examples of how oscillators work with other signals, the role of oscillators in reversal and confirmation, and a concluding chapter about oscillators and what they reveal in continuation signals.

The purpose is to offer practical information that can be applied to improve the timing of trades and to avoid losses caused by poor timing or by overlooking what the signals reveal, especially in the case of momentum oscillators. This book is meant to provide guidance for putting oscillators to work. The basics of oscillators are widely available online, but finding information beyond "what is it" may be more elusive. This book provides you with this next step, the "how to use it" discussion of momentum.

PART I

The Theory of Overbought
and Oversold

CHAPTER 1

Momentum in the Concept of Technical Analysis

Overview: The science of technical analysis is based on estimates, an understanding of probability, and articulation of how current price patterns may translate to future price movement. Because it is an inexact science, technical analysis has been criticized as invalid or unreliable. However, when the alternatives are considered—namely, accepting market averages as the best possible outcome—technical analysis has been demonstrably legitimized time and again.

The purpose behind a range of analyses collectively termed "technical analysis" is to accomplish three goals. First, technical signals define the most recent price behavior and its associated risks. Second, they enable the analyst to study current prices of a stock or other security and to use charts to identify what is occurring today. Third, these signals provide a setup for possible future movement of price within a current trend, enabling prediction of what is likely to occur next.

The future price movement is of greatest interest to the technicians, who consider entering a trade in order to exploit and profit from the likely movement expected to occur. The higher the technician's confidence level (based on strength of identified signals), the more likely price will behave in the manner expected. This points to a concern every trader should have about prediction: Technical analysis does not provide certainty about future price movement. The best any trader can hope for is the *likely* next move in price based on signals. These come in the form of price, volume, moving averages, and momentum. Far too many traders come to believe that price can be predicted accurately, and they act accordingly. A more enlightened view recognizes that using technical signals of many forms will improve the likely outcomes of profitable timing and reduce the future losses to be experienced. This is the goal in technical analysis and the use of signals.

Traders may fall into the trap of applying false assumptions to the market, and to acting according to those assumptions rather than to fact. One of the most common of these assumptions is that the price at which stock is bought is a "zero" point, and that future price movement will always move higher. Even though this is an unsound assumption, it is present in many cases. Why buy stock unless you believe it will increase in value?

Traders must apply rational thought to the process of entering a position. If the timing is poor, no degree of technical analysis can make it a better decision or offset the timing element. With this in mind, analysis should begin *before* shares are purchased. The purchase price is not "zero" but part of a continuum of ever-changing prices, potentially moving higher but also potentially moving lower. Few traders apply technical tests to a company or its stock before the purchase. A wise question to ask before buying is: What are the technical attributes of this stock and is this a good point to make a purchase?

If a stock's price has been rising for several months, is it too late to buy shares today? Will the price continue to rise or is it overdue for a correction? Most investors do not ask this question; they see a positive trend underway and they want to get into the position to benefit from the continued popularity of the stock. But what do the technical signals reveal?

A basic understanding of price, volume, moving averages, and the signals involved may easily point to good or bad timing for a trade. An investor may review the status of the signals based on these characteristics before making trade, although most traders do not perform critical analysis before trading. Moving beyond these basic price signals, momentum oscillators provide insight into the current trend that does not show up in other signals. Momentum, because it measures the speed and strength of price movement, reveals a lot. Its study shows when momentum is growing and when it is beginning to slow down. If momentum is slowing down, it anticipates a price decline to follow. In this situation, buying shares of stock would be poorly timed. It makes more sense to buy when a price has declined with strong momentum, the momentum has slowed down but more recently, price has stopped falling and begun rising, and momentum has started to rise as well. At this point—the bottom of the momentum well—most traders are fearful of further decline and will not be willing to buy more shares. However, this is the exact moment when a wise trader—acting as a contrarian—recognizes the opportunity and acts.

Decline in price is not enough information to time trades. You also need to see the turn in momentum. Because momentum is not concerned with price direction, the timing for a buy decision is easily spotted. Most traders are not looking for this moment because they focus only on price and look for reversal signals related to price alone. However, with a price decline, momentum slows down to a low point; and then it begins to increase as price stops falling. This is the perfect time to buy, although a majority of traders will not act until a new bullish trend has been well established. At that point, momentum points out likely future price movement, and with the conditions better understood with momentum analysis, timing of new trades is potentially well timed.

Near-future price movement may consist of three possible outcomes. A *reversal* occurs when a trend's direction changes and price begins a new trend in the opposite direction (or in a consolidation, a sideways-moving trend). A *continuation* occurs when the current trend continues to evolve. And a *retracement* is an adjustment to most recent price movement to off-set excessive or exaggerated changes in price levels. Most traders focus on reversal. The desire to anticipate price movement and enter or exit trades with perfect timing leads to a desire to track signals with this singular goal in mind. In this approach, continuation signals are often ignored entirely or their value is discounted. And retracement is widely misunderstood. It is not reversal, but movement in price to correct exaggerated or extreme past price behavior. Misinterpreting retracement as reversal leads to many errors in timing.

Fortunately, the mistakes traders make in misreading signals can be managed and their effects reduced. Using momentum to confirm what other signals appear to indicate allows traders to add a secondary observation before taking a current trade. Momentum may also provide opposite information, a divergence from what price or volume indicates. When this occurs, momentum tends to have greater influence on future price behavior and should be given greater weight than other signals.

All technical analysis is designed to identify these price patterns and behavior and to anticipate what will be likely to occur next. The subtle part of this is in how traders combine signals of different types to better understand the complexity and unpredictable nature of price trends and behavior.

An Overview of Technical Analysis

The nature of technical analysis (and the role of momentum) is poorly understood. It is a mysterious thing. Few market experts can explain *why* prices may rise strongly for years, only to collapse in a dash of bearish decline. This is explained away as merely cyclical or the result of excessive speculation in past months or years. In fact, however, it is a combination of matters. Prices move due to understandable market conditions, and this is where momentum plays a role.

To make a comparison, in the housing market, prices tend to rise in most years, and a speculator may be willing to pay a higher price this year than last year, on the belief that prices will rise once again. That speculator may even borrow additional funds to increase holdings in more properties, and with this leveraged position, profits will be ever higher as prices rise again and again. It may be observed that in this condition— with higher prices each year—the speculator is correct in the assumption … until he is wrong. At some point, prices will correct. The market will be overbought and values inflated, so that in some uncertain time span, the entire market will correct itself. Prices will flatten out or fall, and the overextended speculator may lose everything.

What happened here? Momentum.

The market for real estate grows year after year on strong momentum. Speculation fuels more construction because prices rise more rapidly every year. At some point, the supply becomes greater than the demand, and the market collapses.

Could this have been foreseen? Yes. As the market begins to peak, the keen observer will notice that the time on the market (days required for a house to sell) begins to increase. The inventory of homes for sell begins edging upward. Offers begin to decline below asking price. And yet, developers continue building more homes every month.

Those easily recognized signals—time on the market, inventory of homes, and the spread (difference between asking price and selling price)—are all signals. As they change, it signals a slowing down of momentum. This is always the first sign that the bullish real estate market is peaking and soon will plateau or even decline.

The same observation may be applied to the stock market. A slowing of momentum is the first sign that the current trend will soon be exhausted. This first sign may then lead to other signals in price, volume, and moving averages to spot the reversal point. These technical signals are easily found, but the starting point is momentum.

This raises a question: If momentum is so valuable, why doesn't everyone use it (in real estate, the stock market, or elsewhere)? There are two reasons. As market advances, what Federal Reserve Chairman Alan Greenspan called "irrational exuberance blinds speculators and prevents them from recognizing the slowing momentum that foreshadows decline." Greenspan was referring to the infamous dot.com bubble, but it applies to all market movements. Momentum leads the way.

This clearly works as markets advance. As prices price quickly on strong momentum, a growing number of traders enter, peaking as the market tops. Those late entering traders tend to lose because they buy at the top, exactly the wrong point in the momentum curve.

The same tendency is seen as markets decline. Momentum applies to strength and speed of price movement, but not to direction. A high-momentum decline in prices could be called "irrational pessimism" to modify Greenspan's term for rising markets. Those holding shares tend to sell out of panic as prices continue declining, and fail to recognize that the strength of momentum eventually declines. The downward spiral slows down, plateaus at the bottom, and then turns to the upside. The change in momentum is the early warning signal of a change in the trend. It occurs before price begins a strong reversal.

The second reason that more traders ignore momentum is that they do not understand its nature. Many traders are aware of momentum oscillators, but tend to think of them as esoteric variations of price signals. They do not know how to interpret momentum. They expect it to act as confirmation only, but rarely consider it as a leading indicator. The lack of understanding among investors means that the power and strength of oscillators is largely ignored in the market; it also means that the timing of trades is not executed very well because of this lack of application.

The oscillator is much more than a variation of reversal signals, as many investors and traders think. Within the larger body of technical analysis, many different forms of signals make this a rich science, but one that is poorly understood.

The Range of Technical Signals

The range of technical analysis consists of several different signals. The most relied upon of these is the price signal. This may consist of traditional *Western* technical indicators such as double tops or bottoms, head and shoulders, triangles and wedges, flags and pennants, breakouts from the existing trading range, or gaps. There are many different forms of Western technical price signals, and these are valuable in spotting reversal as well as continuation of price.

Signals may also appear in the form of *Eastern* technical signals, also called Japanese candlestick signals. There are dozens of reversal and continuation candlesticks, and when used in conjunction with other signals, they may provide exceptional forecasts of the next price movement within the trend. Although most traders rely on candlestick charts, many do not understand or recognize specific signals. They may also fail to understand the varying degrees of reliability among different signals. Not all candlestick signals are equally reliable, and this points to the need to study candlesticks and to observe them on charts to spot the occurrence and the resulting changes in price.

Beyond price are several nonprice technical signals. Volume indicators may consist of a single spike, a session in which volume is exceptionally high and, by definition, retreats immediately to more typical levels. Volume indicators are based on collecting and analyzing daily high, low, opening, and closing prices. Many additional signals based on volume result in indicators used by many traders. These study the moving averages of upward-moving price sessions versus downward-moving price sessions; the degree of change in volume on these sessions; or combinations of volume and price. By themselves, volume indicators are difficult to interpret and are subject to interpretation. When added to other signals and used to confirm what is predicted, volume indicators are of greater value. However, the most basic of these—the volume spike—is the strongest volume-based indicator, which often occurs at the point of price reversal and may be further confirmed by momentum oscillators. By definition, a "spike" is a single day (or 2 days) of unusually high trading volume, followed immediately by a return to more typical levels. This is distinguished from a volume trend, when volume increases or decreases from day to day.

Moving averages are a third form of technical analysis. These are averages of prices for the most recent trading sessions. Moving averages are lagging indicators and, by themselves, are not normally reliable for predicting the future. However, when sets of moving averages are employed together, the various crossovers and convergences between averages and price provide strong confirmation of other signals. For example, as two different moving averages converge and then cross over one another, it may represent a reversal signal; and when the moving averages cross above or below price, the same signal may be taken from this. However, when these are confirmed by other signals, notably in momentum oscillators, they take on greater strength and importance.

Finally, momentum oscillators complete the range of signals within technical analysis. Momentum is articulated through several different oscillators, or calculations based on advancing and declining prices and identification of conditions Within midrange indicates that prices are reasonable at current levels. Overbought reveals that a reversal or retracement should be expected to take prices down and back to midrange. And oversold reveals that reversal or retracement is likely to the upside. All the oscillator ranges are determined by a series of averages over time.

Returning to the example of the real estate market, momentum can be measured by rising or falling prices, time on the market, inventory of homes for sale, and the spread between asking and selling price. All these indicators reveal conditions in the market; the change in these indicators reveals whether momentum is rising or falling. The same is true within the stock market. Momentum is easily measured in terms of whether price is rising or falling too rapidly and becoming overbought or oversold. These conditions are leading indicators and will be followed by adjustments in price and its direction of movement.

The Controversy: Does Technical Analysis Work?

The great market controversy is whether technical analysis works. To many, it is the key to swing trading and to the timing of trades, the science of trading profitably. To others, it is an unreliable system that does not provide insight into near-future price movement.

For those who do not believe in technical analysis, the facts are stubborn things. A review of the many technical signals in the form of price, volume, moving averages, and momentum demonstrate that price can be anticipated and acted upon as long as the key elements are present. These include the following:

1. *Proximity.* The technical signals found on stock charts take dozens of forms, but it is not only the signal, but where it is located, that matters. Most reversal signals are likely to be found close to resistance at the top of the trading range or at support at the bottom.

2. *Strong signals.* The stronger the signal, the higher the trader's confidence. The proximity of reversal signals is augmented when price also gaps (above resistance or below support). Price gaps are not only strong indicators, but also found as parts of multisession reversal signals.

3. *Confirmation.* The reversal signal should never be acted upon by itself. Equally strong confirmation is required in the form of another signal indicating the same likely price movement to follow.

4. *Smart risk management.* No signals are going to provide 100 percent confidence. However, by following the previous guidelines, confidence can be extremely high, and timing made as reliable as possible. Even so, smart risk management means limiting the capital placed at risk. By exposing the same level of capital, for every trade, losses will not be devastating. And every trader will experience losses. The key is to increase the likelihood of profits, not to guarantee profits in every trade.

Analysis as a Means for Timing Trades

Most traders in the market are crowd followers. They act in accordance with what other traders are doing, and their decision-making process is emotional. As prices rise, traders become greedy and enter positions in the expectation of greater profits to follow. As prices fall, traders panic and close positions. In both cases, the decision is entirely emotional.

An alternative is found in contrarian investing. The contrarian observes the emotional tendencies of "crowd thinking" and resists acting out of greed or panic. The majority most often is wrong in their timing. Instead of following the advice to "buy low and sell high," they do the exact opposite. They "buy high and sell low." That is what greed and panic cause.

The contrarian relies on logic and analysis to time trades. This is not always a simple process to follow. Moving against the majority is not an easy step to take, but experience shows that contrarians outperform the market by relying on chart signals and not on emotion.

Momentum and Other Signals (Price, Volume, and Moving Averages)

Where do signals fit into the timing picture? In technical analysis, it is all about how signals are used, not in isolation but as a unified procedure. Momentum measures the strength or weakness of trends, but not the direction. A momentum indicator provides guidelines and demonstrates when a trend has moved too far in either direction.

Supplementing momentum are other technical signals. Price signals track the trend and price behavior and show a trader the ever-changing levels of volatility in stocks and options.

Volume is another form of confirmation. As volume increases or decreases over a period of days, it may act as a confirming signal of big movements to follow. The volume spike is an exceptionally strong reversal confirmation. When it occurs at the same time as a price signal, it normally means it is time to act.

Moving averages, even as lagging indicators, exhibit some characteristics that confirm price reversal. Convergence and divergence are among these, as well as price crossover.

Key Concepts

The stock market is not as mysterious as many observers think. It is true that there are no magic formulas to get rich in the market. Success requires hard work. Technical analysis is of value, but only if it is recognized as an analytical tool to improve the instances of well-timed trades and not as the magic elixir for accumulating wealth without effort.

The key concepts behind technical analysis are as follows:

1. Technical analysis puts price behavior in context, describes current price activity, and points to likely future price movement.
2. Three forms of price movement are of great interest in technical analysis. These are reversal, continuation, and retracement.
3. Price indicators take two forms. Western technical indicators are based on overall price patterns, and Eastern (candlestick) indicators develop from a series of daily session patterns.
4. Volume, moving averages, and momentum accompany and confirm price indicators.
5. Technical analysis relies on four attributes: proximity, strength of signals, strength of confirmation, and risk management.
6. Most traders act emotionally, buying out of greed and selling out of panic. Contrarian traders resist emotion and base timing of trades on analysis and logic.

Class Questions for Discussion and/or Mini-Case Studies

Multiple choice

1. Technical analysis enables traders to
   (a) distinguish between bullish and bearish trends
   (b) track trends and determine whether they are long term or short term
   (c) identify the strength and duration of trends, but not the direction
   (d) use lagging indicators to spot weakening of current price movement
2. Three forms of price movement are
   (a) reversal, continuation, and retracement
   (b) bullish, bearish, and neutral
   (c) long term, short term, and volatile
   (d) gapping, sideways, and strong

3. Price indicators are confirmed by

   (a) other price indicators alone

   (b) momentum alone

   (c) volume, moving averages, and momentum

   (d) Western and Eastern signals alone

Discussion

Select a price chart and identify

   (a) points of reversal and confirmation

   (b) trends with signals of coming reversal

   (c) especially strong reversal signals

    Discuss the level of confidence when signals occur, and whether the signals are strong enough to justify entering a trade.

CHAPTER 2

The Concept of Overbought and Oversold

Overview: Momentum is based on price averages, but even as a lagging indicator, the calculated status of price as overbought or oversold informs traders about likely points of reversal. As a mechanism for confirmation of other signals and for trade timing, momentum measures the speed and strength of price movement and identifies points in a short-term trend where price is most likely to retrace.

Anyone who has ridden a bicycle down a hill knows all about momentum. You coast along as you pick up speed. Then, when the downhill turns to uphill, the speed slows down. Eventually the bicycle will stop.

This is one form of momentum.

Traders know this, of course, but too often they forget to apply this knowledge in the way that they analyze a stock chart and price behavior. The essential point to remember is

Momentum measures the speed and strength of price movement, but not the direction.

This reality is confusing in a sense because momentum also identifies when price has moved "too far," meaning into an overbought situation at the top of the price range or an oversold condition at the bottom. As a visual aid to identifying turning points in price, momentum appears to reflect directional tendencies (bullish or bearish). In fact, the movement of a momentum oscillator above or below a mid-range point is interpreted as bullish or bearish, but only because price has moved excessively. In such times, it is likely to reverse and then move in the opposite direction, a symptom of both price and momentum.

This is a seemingly contradictory attribute of momentum. It does not determine the direction that price moves, but it signals when it has moved too far to the top (overbought) or to the bottom (oversold). However, these signals are not contradictory. It is true that momentum measures the speed and strength of price movement, but not the direction. This is a form of taking the temperature of the trend. And it makes perfect sense that a condition will be "over" the assumed normal price range. When price moves too high too quickly, it is overbought as a reflection of momentum, and when it moves too low too quickly, it is oversold.

Overbought/Oversold as a Symptom of Momentum

The index used in any momentum oscillator identifies when price has moved too far. In other words, the momentum of a balanced price chart should remain in that middle trading range, and when it moves above or below, an adjustment is likely to occur. This is determined by the index created by the momentum oscillator. The calculation is intended to measure how momentum works at any given time, based on how quickly price moves. The oscillator may be thought of as a speedometer. Just as a car's speed is measured in miles per hour, the car may be going too fast or too slow, rather than moving with the flow of traffic. Momentum acts in the same way as a measurement of stock price behavior. Is its change in price "normal" and "reasonable" or is it exceeding expectations in either direction?

These expectations relate to the interaction between forces in the market (supply and demand for shares) versus the reasonable measurement of price. This occurs through the price/earnings ratio (PE), for example. Price is divided by earnings per share to arrive at the current multiple. This represents the number of years of earnings in the price. For example, if price is $35.65 per share and the most recent earnings per share was $1.45, PE is 24.6. The current price per share of $35.65 represents 24.6 years of earnings, based on current earnings levels. The PE is generally thought to be reasonable if it is between 10 and 25, so if the PE moves above 25, it is viewed as overpriced.

When this occurs, it may be reflected in a momentum oscillator. For example, if price increased to $46 per share, and the latest earnings remains at \$1.45 per share, PE becomes 31.7 (\$46 ÷ \$1.45). That is beyond the expected moderate range, meaning the stock is overpriced. This is likely to be reflected in momentum as an overbought condition. As price moves higher too quickly, calculated momentum will move into overbought (to the upside); as price moves lower too quickly, momentum moves into oversold (to the downside).

The value in this tendency is that the rebalancing always occurs. The study of any price chart over time proves this. Price does not remain overbought or oversold for long. Once the oscillator moves into the overbought or oversold range, the correction is usually immediate. When price remains outside of the mid-range for more than two or three sessions, it is unusual.

The measurement of price behavior through momentum reveals as a first point when price has moved too far, too fast. However, another aspect, often overlooked, is the speed of change. In viewing the index line of an oscillator, in some cases the move toward the borders of overbought or oversold is slow; in other cases, it is fast and extreme. This rapid momentum reflects strength in the price trend and reveals a second important attribute of momentum:

> *The rate of momentum in one direction is likely to be matched*
> *by an equal rate of speed in the other direction.*

After an oscillator's index rises quickly toward overbought and then moves above the line, the turn and retreat is likely to be just as rapid. The same tendency is seen in oversold conditions, with price retreating above the low levels. Momentum itself—the combination of speed and degree of movement—is not one or the other attribute, but both together. To the astute analyst, this combined set of attributes reveals degrees of likelihood in a reversal.

Analysts must look at not only the overbought and oversold conditions, but where the momentum index resides and how it is trending. Is the index value between 50 and 70 (in generally bullish territory) or is it between 30 and 50 (bearish)? This further helps in deciding whether momentum favors one side over the other. Even though momentum does not measure direction, it is reasonable to quantify momentum in bullish or bearish terms.

Taking this further, how is the momentum index line moving? Is it trending higher or lower? It is a mistake to only look for overbought or oversold conditions, and to ignore the indicator when the index stays in the middle (which it does most of the time). But you can also spot trends by tracking (a) which side of the index dominates and (b) which direction the index is moving. These improve the value of momentum analysis by enabling you to anticipate possible future moves into overbought or oversold.

How Momentum Relates to Price

There is a direct connection between momentum and price. However, a price trend and momentum are not always going to be observed as a perfect match, and often reflect divergence. This occurs because the leading or lagging indicator found in momentum is not going to track price precisely enough to generate an immediate cause and effect.

Momentum is a lagging indicator. Price averages that make up the formula of momentum occur before momentum appears, so this makes sense. However, it is also possible for momentum to serve as a leading indicator, especially in times when price movement has been greatly exaggerated. For example, after an earnings surprise, price often gaps higher (positive surprise) or lower (negative surprise). You know that this overreaction is likely to reverse and for price to move back into range. But when does that begin?

In a situation such as this—gaps in price above resistance or below support—look to momentum as a first signal of a coming change. At the time of price exaggeration, several signals probably appear together. These include volume spikes, price gaps violating the established trading range, continued runaway gaps in the same direction, and of course momentum above the overbought value or below the oversold value. However, momentum is likely to lead the reversal. Once the index value begins retreating into range, price is likely to follow very quickly.

This cause and effect is by no means reliable. It varies in each case. However, as one of many methods for timing entry and exit in a short-term trade or as a reaction to fast price movement, momentum should be tracked to identify those two attributes: speed of change and degree of change.

A Study of Momentum Signals and Market Theories (EMH and RMH)

A theory of how price behaves must address momentum in terms of two aspects: an efficient market and random market. For those who do not believe in the value of technical analysis, these two theories attempt to explain why it is impossible for traders to outperform the market. Both theories are easily disproven and shown to be unrealistic.

The efficient market hypothesis (EMH) is misunderstood even among experienced analysts. The normal assumption is that EMH claims accuracy in current price levels because of the underlying EMH statement:

The price of a security is efficient because it is discounted immediately for all known information in the market, and about the company and its stock.

This does not mean the price is accurate, but merely efficient in how information is taken into the security's price. The hypothesis further does not make any distinction between different types of information (hard facts such as earnings vs. unproven rumor or gossip). It also fails to assign any weight to information. For example, a positive earnings report in which revenue and earnings greatly exceed expectations is "hard" information of great value; but the announced acquisition of a minor competitor is relatively "soft" and probably will not have an equal impact on price behavior.

An "efficient" market reflects the way that various forms of information are considered within the price. This is not the same as current price levels reflecting the value of a company efficiently.

EMH is junk science as applied. It is true that information is considered efficiently, but the name of the theory is unfortunate. It implies that the market is efficient when, in fact, the market is notoriously chaotic and inefficient. Ironically, the efficiency of taking information into account adds to the chaos of the market. Without being able to make a distinction between accurate and inaccurate information, efficiency is a distant hope that cannot be realized. This makes the point that in order to anticipate price behavior, reliance on indicators like momentum makes sense. Momentum analysis is a powerful weapon for navigating the inefficiency of the market.

A related idea, the random walk hypothesis (RWH) puts forth the idea that price movement cannot be consistently predicted by traders, because of the random nature of the market. RWH proposes the nature of the market:

Price movement is entirely random. Therefore, prices cannot be forecast reliably or predicted with any degree of certainty.

Under this theory, price movement will tend to rise or fall arbitrarily. Combined, the efficiency of information and the randomness of price movement present a dismal picture. Under EMH, the current price is deemed to be efficient, so traders may not locate bargain pricing. Under RWH, the market is entirely random, so movement up or down is a 50/50 probability.

Both EMH and RWH can be tested using momentum. What you discover is a reality that is startling to anyone starting out with belief in either of these theories. Momentum as a short-term indicator is far more efficient than market information, broadly speaking. It tests price and volume average movement over time and predicts (or reacts to) exaggerations in price based on information. This is especially true when information is dubious or when price itself overreacts to earnings surprises and other unexpected announcements. The price behavior demonstrates that short-term price is not efficient in any sense, because it does not distinguish between strong and weak information. The market is not random either. An earnings surprise presents a highly reliable likely set of changes. First, price will overreact to the surprise; second, it will self-correct in most instances.

Another way to test EMH and RWH is simply to observe stock charts. Short-term volatility dominates price behavior and is anything but efficient. In fact, the short-term market is extremely chaotic and unpredictable. It is not efficient by any test of that theory. If the market were truly random, trends could not develop. On average, half of daily sessions would show rising prices and the other half would fall. This would be a statistical reality. Under RWH, the market is like a coin toss. On average, half come up heads and half come up tails. This is defied by the development of often lengthy trends in one direction or the other and to rising

prices over many years for well-managed companies with strong fundamentals. How can anyone explain RWH as a realistic proposition?

Both EMH and RWH are reassuring to those who want certainty in
the world. But for anyone who trades in the market, both ideas must be
resisted. If they were true, there would be no reason to trade. You might
as well play roulette and place your entire portfolio value on red or black.
In practice, investors recognize that well-managed companies have strong
fundamentals, and these create strong technical signals with prices rising
over time. Likewise, poorly managed companies see weak fundamentals
and weak technical signals, with prices falling over time. This makes sense
because the market rewards competitive strength and good management,
and punishes weakness.

The reality of the market can be discovered in the inefficiency of price
behavior and in the predictable (nonrandom) nature of momentum.

Applying Momentum to Trade Timing

The nonefficient and nonrandom nature of price behavior are both
reflected immediately in momentum, and this momentum is measured
by a set of momentum oscillators. This should come as no surprise to
anyone who has studied price charts and witnessed the tendency of price
to behave in an inefficient manner, and to predictably (nonrandomly)
act in a particular manner based on evolving circumstances, as well as to
specific reversal or continuation signals; the price behavior in proximity
to resistance and support; and the actual momentum of price over time.
An example makes this point.

The 3-month chart of Caterpillar (CAT) is shown in Figure 2.1. On
April 24, earnings for the quarter ending in March were reported, with
a 33.65 percent positive earnings surprise. On July 30, earnings for the
quarter ending in June were reported, with an 11.65 percent positive
earnings surprise.

The first earnings report took price from the $140 to $145 level up to
the high $150 range. However, the second positive earnings surprise was
followed by a 10-point decline before a strong bullish move occurred. The
momentum indicator [relative strength index (RSI)] identifies points of
oversold and overbought on the chart.

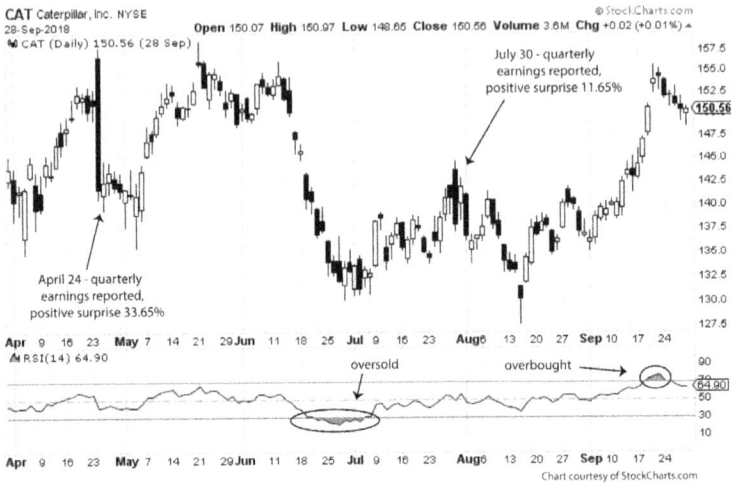

Figure 2.1 Positive earnings surprises

However, taking this chart forward, price declined steeply followed by a bullish reversal signal in momentum. This is shown in Figure 2.2.

This chart revealed downward price behavior concluding with a substantial downward exhaustion gap. However, the most interesting development on this chart was the strong move of RSI into oversold. The previous price gap was dwarfed by the new series of upward gaps

Figure 2.2 Momentum-based reversal signal

taking place after the momentum showed price as oversold. This decline deep into oversold serves as a clear reversal signal. As anticipated, price quickly moved up from a low of $112 per share to $140 by the end of the period shown.

A short-term trade based on the large gap and move in RSI to oversold would have resulted in excellent timing for the bullish reversal—based primarily on the price gaps and on momentum. The sudden and rapid move in price below support by themselves represents strong bullish signals. However, the strongest confirmation on this chart is found in the momentum oscillator, RSI. (See a more detailed discussion of RSI in Chapter 4.)

At first glance, most analysts would not react to RSI's move because it had not moved into "oversold" until the large price drop. However, the RSI oscillator reveals something else of great interest. Note the activity of the stock, appearing to be in a strong downtrend in the month of October. If price continued moving downward, there was no reason to expect a reversal. However, during the final week of October, price stopped trending downward and established a point of support at $112 per share. This often occurs when a trend is exhausted and about to reverse. This was confirmed by RSI at the same time. RSI declined during the month from the top of the middle range down to the oversold level.

This trend in momentum was revealing, but easily overlooked. It demonstrated how the endless interaction within the momentum index anticipates price change. It could be argued that momentum merely reflects price averages; however, the same trend was not seen in the remainder of the chart, when RSI remained in mid-range until the conclusion of the chart.

This is one example of how momentum tracks price over time and measures the strength or weakness of a trend. You can spot reversal signals and strong confirmation, but without also tracking momentum, you cannot know when the adjustment will occur.

The Power of Momentum

The previous example demonstrates some interesting realities about chart analysis and the role of momentum. Starting with the assumptions in the common market theories, the analysis disproves both EMH and RWH. This example of an earnings surprise is by no means rare; in fact, in most instances involving earnings surprises, you are going to find price behavior that first moves in an exaggerated manner and then retreats. The challenge here is not whether price will behave in this manner, but when the reversal will occur. Timing is the great variable, and momentum is the key to identifying the timing of price reaction.

The earnings surprise was "efficiently" reflected in price. However, the counter move to follow was less certain. This means that the market in the case of earnings surprises is anything but efficient. This also makes the point about the value of hard and soft information. An earnings surprise is a form of hard information. However, an efficient discounting of the surprise would be reflected in an *appropriate* level of price behavior. At least, you would expect this to occur in the interest of efficiency. Instead, price moves in an exaggerated fashion because of the tendency of traders to make decisions emotionally. In comparison, the cold, logical contrarian sits back and observes the overreaction and then times a contrary trade to profit from the market inefficiency.

Because this pattern of exaggerated price movement followed by adjustment is so predictable, it makes the RWH equally questionable. There certainly are examples of random price behavior, but it is by no means universal.

Momentum oscillators are far from mysterious. However, applying what they reveal to the timing of trades goes far beyond identifying overbought and oversold conditions. It requires a more in-depth study of both price and momentum. Moving averages—the subject of the next chapter—are usually described as a form of indicator distinct and separate from all others. However, when studied as an attribute of momentum, moving averages take on a more predictive role in anticipating price behavior.

Momentum and Default Settings

Many traders track momentum as part of their process, but they change the default settings of oscillators. The explanation usually is that by changing defaults, more signals are generated. The desire for more signals is understandable; however, if those signals are false, then they will mislead a trader and result in ill-timed trades.

For example, by analyzing RSI, which is examined in depth in Chapter 4, a chart can be adjusted to demonstrate both the value of default settings and the danger of adjusting those settings. Figure 2.3 displays a chart with the default of 14 sessions (the price average used in RSI).

In this chart, momentum as measured by RSI remains between the index values of 30 and 70. No signals are produced, although the index touches the borders momentarily on several occasions. A trader receives no signals from this regarding momentum because the index never moves to overbought or oversold.

A trader should take reassurance from the lack of signals, because it gives no warnings of price behavior that may create problems in the immediate future. However, a trader desiring more signals may change the default. For example, what happens if the 14-session default is changed to 8 sessions? It is likely that many more signals will emerge, as shown in Figure 2.4.

A trader desiring a higher number of signals will certainly be pleased with these results. The chart with these adjusted settings yielded four instances of momentum moving into oversold and one instance of

Figure 2.3 Default settings, 14 periods

Figure 2.4 Adjusted settings, 8 periods

overbought. Although some of these were accurate, they were mild signals and did not provide strong reversal indication. Two of the oversold
signals, highlighted on the chart, were false signals. A trader acting as the
result of these signals would have taken a bullish trade, but it would have
been badly timed. A bullish reversal did not occur.

The change in default setting led to false signals. A problem in this
observation is that with more signals produced, some were valid, but very
short term, and others were false. How can you tell the difference?

Because default settings were adjusted, it is impossible to tell whether
a signal is true or false. In the example, 2 of the 5 (40 percent) were false
signals. In other words, an oscillator is developed and assigned default
settings for good reasons. In the case of RSI, the use of 14 sessions was the
result of testing and comparison, concluding that it was the most reliable
basis for the oscillator. The desire to discover more signals, just for the
same of having more to act upon, is misguided. If more signals include
a high incidence of false signals, then adjusting the default is ill-advised.

The next chapter addresses overbought and oversold conditions from
another perspective. Confirming what oscillators reveal can be expanded
through the observation of moving averages, especially when two averages
of different duration are studied together and overlaid on a stock chart.

The convergence between those averages, and crossover with price, add to the predictive value of momentum oscillators.

Class Questions for Discussion and/or Mini-Case Studies

Multiple Choice

1. Momentum can be defined as a measurement of
   (a) the speed and strength of price movement, but not the direction
   (b) strength of a bullish or bearish price trend and proof it will continue
   (c) reversal and likelihood of a price move in the opposite direction
   (d) volume in daily trading and how it affects price
2. Overbought and oversold conditions indicate
   (a) the reliability of price reversal signals
   (b) that stock is priced too high
   (c) that price has moved too far and is likely to retrace
   (d) imperfections in the market
3. EMH is the
   (a) expected movement height
   (b) efficient market hypothesis
   (c) exponential mood holdover
   (d) extrinsic median hunch
4. The RWH is a belief that
   (a) all price movement is predictable
   (b) the market cannot be predicted
   (c) EMH is incorrect
   (d) technical analysis is the foundation of the market

Discussion

Analyze a stock chart and look for examples of RWH in practice. Explain how RWH dictates price behavior of stocks. Present pro and con arguments based on what the chart reveals.

CHAPTER 3

Moving Averages

Overview: The moving average (MA) is a lagging indicator, which limits its value in predicting future price movement. However, when the behavior of two MAs with different timeframes is studied, the tendency for convergence and crossover adds value and creates confirmation value when compared to momentum trends. Crossovers between MAs and from MA to price have significance; and MA movement can further be used to track resistance and support.

The moving average (MA) is a commonly seen attribute of stock charts. However, is this truly a price indicator? Or is it more valuable when used along with momentum oscillators? The distinction is worth studying. Most chartists consider MA as a price indicator. However, when used solely regarding price, MA is a lagging indicator. It consists of price alone and, by nature, is completely backward-looking. The value is minimized because historical price activity cannot accurately predict future price activity.

However, when a combination of two MA signals is overlaid on a price chart, the activity of those MA lines reflects momentum in several ways. When thought of not as a price indicator, but as a momentum signal, MA takes on value in confirming what is taking place in the evolution of price and volatility.

In fact, MA is more than just the ultimate lagging indicator, because of its reflection of price over time. Value is added to MA when used as part of a comprehensive series of signals and confirmation. The best known use of MA is the combined 50-day and 200-day on a price chart. Great value is assigned to crossovers and convergence. The crossover takes two forms. First is a crossover between the two MA lines; second is the crossover of MA and price. In both cases, a reversal signal can be confirmed; as a momentum indicator, crossover in MA often occurs before price reverses.

The Concept of Crossover

MAs cross one another as a factor of price trends. However, the significance of a crossover depends on several factors: momentum of the change in MA (convergence), proximity to resistance or support, and proximity of MA to current price. This reveals that with MA, a lot more is going on than just price averages. Because the latest entries in MAs are of greater importance than remote sessions, the current crossover action reveals that price trends are growing in strength or diminishing. These are momentum attributes in both directions.

Proximity is a second feature in MA analysis, often ignored by traders or at least not recognized. Most reversal activity is going to take place at or near resistance or support. An MA crossover at these critical price points is strong confirmation that a reversal is coming in the very near future. When a crossover between MA and price occurs, it adds strength to the crossover of one MA line to the other.

All these basic ideas are easily observed on price charts. This chapter demonstrates the value of MA crossover and other features, not as confirmation of price behavior, but as confirmation or forecasting of momentum.

Analysts point to crossover (one MA moving above or below another) as a bullish or bearish price signal. However, the frequency of this occurrence without dependable result in price behavior makes price-related MA signals less reliable than most other types of signals. However, when MA signals are viewed along with changes in momentum, the MA trend gains great value.

The first MA signal to be aware of is the basic crossover. When one MA line crosses the other, it produces a signal. In using a 50-day and 200-day MA combination, this is easy to spot. If the shorter MA crosses above the longer, it is considered bullish. For example, the chart of Google in Figure 3.1 shows this type of crossover.

The signal is clear. The crossover of the shorter-term MA above the longer-term MA took place while price jumped. However, because MA is simply a reflection of the price trend, this crossover was caused more by the four rising sessions than by the price gap. This is a preliminary signal, but by itself, this is not enough to generate a new trade. Even if

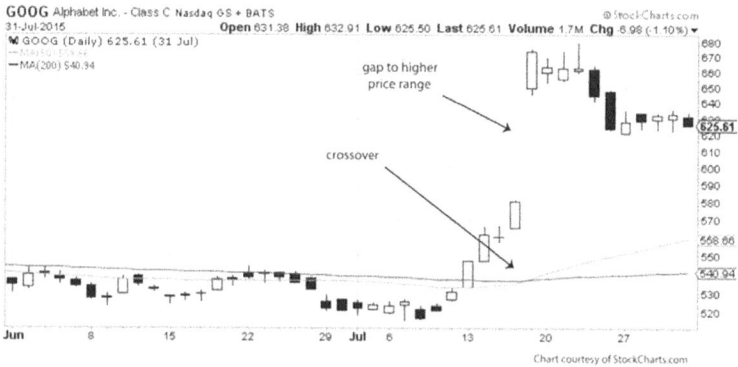

Figure 3.1 Bullish crossover

it were, by the time the crossover was seen, the price would have already moved higher.

Momentum is a better signal for anticipating strong price movement. When the same chart is studied with Bollinger Bands (Chapter 8), the bullish development is more easily spotted. This is shown in Figure 3.2.

The price had been range-bound in a consolidation trend for over a month. On July 13, a 4-day trend moving out of consolidation occurred. However, there was more to this move than just the price direction. The change also took price above the upper band, a significant development. Because the upper and lower bands are two standard deviations away from the middle band, any move of price outside the upper or lower band is significant. In this case, the three sessions after the gap were also above the upper band. This signal, based on momentum, confirms what the bullish

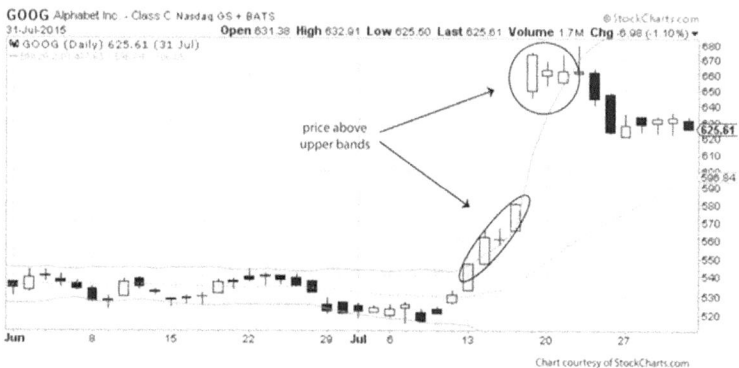

Figure 3.2 Bullish crossover with Bollinger Bands

MA revealed. It adds strength of momentum to the price move, a case in which the MA—combined with Bollinger Bands—was convincing as a breakout signal. The most notable aspect here is that the momentum in the Bollinger Bands occurred before the big price move, so the time to act appeared quickly, but in advance of the price move.

This demonstrates a powerful predictive benefit to MA analysis. However, when studied along with Bollinger Bands and its two standard deviations of outer bands, MA produces an exceptionally strong reversal signal *before* price reverses. This offsets the most common complaint about MA. As a lagging indicator, it has little or no value in a predictive sense. But when two MA lines are shown as they interact with Bollinger Bands, price movement is anticipated, and the reversal signal is strongly indicated.

The same relationship between MA and Bollinger Bands momentum is easily viewed during a bearish change. Figure 3.3 shows a case of a bearish crossover, with the shorter-term MA moving below the longer-term MA.

This development is like the previous one, but with price gapping in the opposite direction. The crossover is a lagging indicator that appeared only after price had gapped well below. This by itself reveals the flaw in MA analysis. Because it is a lagging indicator, the signal is seen too late to act. When analysis is limited to MA crossover, there is no value to be gained. For many criticisms of MA as a signal, this is as far as it goes, and the conclusion is reached that MA cannot be used predictively. This would be true if no additional signaling power could be added to the analysis.

Figure 3.3 Bearish crossover

Figure 3.4 Bearish crossover with Bollinger Bands

When the same chart is studied with Bollinger Bands in support of MA, the move can be anticipated with exceptional reliability. In this instance, MA as a momentum signal is made powerful when added to Bollinger Bands. This effect is shown in Figure 3.4.

The initial price moving below the lower band began on September 28. This 2-day signal also represented the second and third days of a 3-day bearish candlestick continuation signal, the bearish three black lines. This consists of a black session, a downward gap, and then two more black sessions. Continuation signals in the form of candlesticks are often ignored by traders or poorly understood; however, they provide benefits as a form of confirmation that the current trend will not end in the immediate future. Of even greater value, continuation signals confirm what momentum has already predicted.

As a continuation signal, the bearish three black lines forecast that the downward trend previously established is likely to continue; and that the MA and Bollinger Bands in combination were strong and dependable signals. Combined with the Bollinger move below the lower band, it is a strong sign of more downward movement.

Making a move at this first set of signals would be well timed, and this was confirmed after the downward gap by three more sessions below the lower band. No short-term trend lasts forever, as this chart revealed. Once the downward shift occurred, a new reversal appeared. The three sessions appearing immediately after the gap formed a bullish candlestick signal called the morning star (black session, downward gap, white session, upward gap, and a final white session). This indicated good timing to close the bearish move made before the large gap.

This chart provides an excellent example of how momentum—in this case, Bollinger Bands—confirmed what price behavior revealed. The difference, however, is that many forms of momentum anticipate coming price moves. Unlike the lagging nature of MA, for example, Bollinger Bands gives notice of a likely move in price to occur very soon.

Crossovers are worthwhile signals, but by themselves, they show up too late. They also tend to whipsaw. This means that without independent signals, movement of price based only on MA might easily give off a false signal. Therefore, every signal must be confirmed by other signals, including price as well as momentum. As a price signal, MA can be discounted as a lagging indicator; as part of momentum, MA crossover bolsters confidence in what the price trend signals and in what will happen next.

Price Crossovers

The combination of MA and other signals, such as Bollinger Bands, works equally well with the second form of crossover, when price moves above or below both MA lines. The same caution applies in this form of crossover: As with MA crossover between the two lines, the price crossover is a lagging indicator.

Most traders consider MA crossover as a price signal, which is not a reliable price signal. It is a lagging indicator and by the time it has been spotted, it is usually too late to enter a responsive trade. However, when the value of price crossover is reviewed as part of momentum, it takes on significant value as a confirming signal. This is true when momentum is shifting from an overbought to oversold condition, or vice versa; or when a separate MA signal has been found, in which case price crossover is a form of momentum confirmation.

When price moves above the MA lines, it is considered bullish. This is likely to be found when momentum is changing and confirms a price reversal in the same direction. However, it must be viewed in terms of momentum and not as a price signal. In this case, momentum may confirm price, if overbought and oversold conditions are ended as part of the price reversal; but that is a confirming signal, separate from the price crossover. The crossover is significant separately from a price reversal. An example of this is shown in Figure 3.5.

The price crossover was not significant or permanent with the large decline of August 24, as this was part of a marketwide drop in prices. However, on September 1, the single session below the MA lines marked the beginning of the crossover that led to a bullish trend. This was confirmed exactly 1 month later.

In the case of this price crossover, the move signaled a bullish change as price went above resistance. But at that point, would it hold? It would have been impossible to tell based solely on the MA development. When the same chart is studied with momentum in mind, stronger and more convincing bullish signals emerged, combining the crossover with Bollinger Bands. This is shown in Figure 3.6.

Figure 3.5 Bullish price crossover

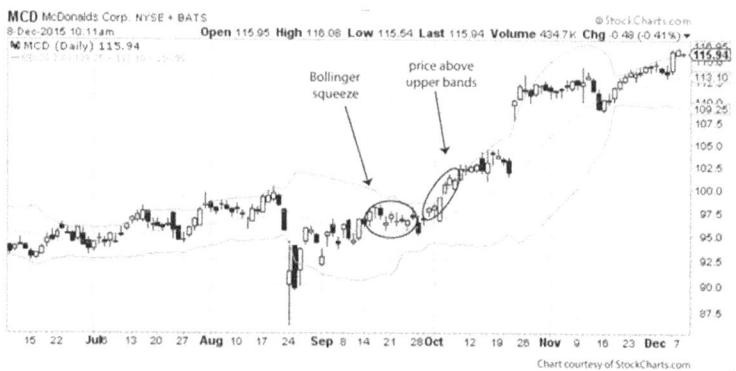

Figure 3.6 Bullish price crossover with Bollinger Bands

In this version of the chart based on Bollinger Bands momentum, two situations developed immediately before the big price move. First was a narrowing of daily trading range in the top half, above the middle band, but below the upper. This is called a Bollinger squeeze and it anticipates a breakout in the same direction (in this case, a bullish move). Second, as price broke out to the upside, it also moved above the upper band over several consecutive sessions. This strongly predicted a bullish move to follow; and the actual move followed 2 weeks later with a large upside gap over 7 points.

This brings up another point about momentum analysis. Price reaction to momentum signals is not always immediate. In this case, an exceptionally strong momentum signal did not see reaction in price until 2 weeks later. Some analysts point to this time span as a sign that the momentum shift was invalid. This is not true. It only points out that cause and effect may be immediate or may take many sessions before results are seen.

Crossover may also confirm itself by moving across both MA lines. This adds strength to the momentum that is observed. An exceptionally strong bearish crossover is highlighted in Figure 3.7.

In this case, the crossover took less than 1 month, but it was easily observed. Even so, until the two-part crossover was complete, this signal by itself was not actionable. To confirm the likelihood of a new, bearish move, the signal found in Bollinger Bands was more compelling. This is shown in Figure 3.8.

What is noteworthy here is the change in daily trading range. In the first half on the chart, price was range-bound in consolidation. The large

Figure 3.7 Bearish price crossover

Figure 3.8 Bearish price crossover with Bollinger Bands

white candlestick took price above the upper band in mid-June, but this did not hold. Rather, it marked the beginning of a more volatile period with more price instability and growing momentum. In fact, the continuation of narrow daily sessions retreated into consolidation after the upward move, and then began to decline. Once price fell below the lower band, the breakout below the support of $65 per share made a strong case for a bearish trend.

These examples reveal the true value of momentum as a leading indicator. MA lags price action, which is by no means mysterious. However, when momentum in its various forms is added to the analysis, you are likely to see a more convincing set of signals that do not follow price behavior but lead it.

Resistance and Support Tracking with MA

Another feature of MA that may be more valuable than providing reversal signals is a tendency for the shorter-term MA to track and confirm both resistance and support. This is normally seen as a track of declining resistance during a downtrend, and of rising support during an uptrend.

For example, the 50MA line tracks a declining resistance trend in the chart in Figure 3.9. This serves a double purpose. First, it confirms dynamic resistance. Compared to the traditional method of marking resistance or support with a straight line, the ability to spot resistance dynamically is clearly an advantage. Second, this chart reveals visually

Figure 3.9 Tracking declining resistance

Figure 3.10 Tracking rising support

the low volatility in the gradual price decline, a sign that momentum was steady and neither increasing nor decreasing. The MA line is surpassed only twice, and in each case for only a single trading session.

The same tendency can be witnessed in the case of rising support. Figure 3.10 provides an example of the 50MA tracking support. The exception to this trend was seen in the marketwide decline of August 24 and the price recovery, which took a full month.

Given the narrow trading range for this stock, MA tracking signaled that no sudden or substantial changes were likely to occur—at least not yet. In this case, momentum was low, so that the established low volatility would be likely to continue. A signal of change would be seen in expanded trading range in daily sessions accompanied by changes in momentum signals well in advance of a strong price move.

Pro and Con of MA Analysis

Momentum comes in many forms and can be applied to effectively set up improved trade timing. When momentum anticipates price trends, it is especially valuable, and that is the point about analysis: identifying signals to anticipate reversals before they occur.

A primary advantage in MA analysis is that it serves as confirmation of what you see in other momentum signals. In this chapter, Bollinger Bands signals were the momentum indicator of choice, and the point was made that MA by itself does not provide useful timely information for price movement; however, when coupled with other signals, MA tends to confirm what momentum forecasts, and the results are witnessed in price formations and responses.

The major disadvantage is in the problem of MA as a lagging indicator, when used only as a price signal. By the time MA signals appear, the move in price has already occurred. However, this disadvantage can be turned to a positive attribute of the confirmation process, and when MA is treated as a momentum signal rather than as a price signal. Locating other momentum signals as well as price and volume reversal (or confirmation) makes MA a valued form of secondary confirmation. This is true whether you rely on candlestick signals, traditional Western signals (such as double tops or bottoms, head and shoulders, or runaway gaps), or strictly the changes in momentum itself. Beyond the basic understanding of MA analysis as crossover signals, coupling MA with other momentum oscillators can vastly improve trade timing.

The next chapter begins Part II of the book, in which specific oscillators are examined and explained in terms of timing trades reliably.

Class Questions for Discussion and/or Mini-Case Studies

Multiple Choice

1. Crossover applies to
   (a) price crossing above or below the MA
   (b) a shorter MA crossing above a longer MA
   (c) a shorter MA crossing below a longer MA
   (d) all of the above

2. Crossover may be described as
   (a) a leading indicator
   (b) a lagging indicator that is of value in confirming other signals
   (c) a lagging indicator of no value in forecasting price movement
   (d) part of the more extensive Bollinger Band signal
3. Crossover is useful in tracking
   (a) rising resistance or falling support
   (b) sideways moving resistance or support
   (c) falling support or rising resistance
   (d) price only, but not resistance or support

Mini-Case study

A company is experiencing growing levels of volatility. This adds to the difficulty of prediction for the next move in price; as a result, knowing when to enter or exit a position is complicated. Find the chart of a company with high volatility and describe how the combined use of two MAs and Bollinger Bands is an aid in improved timing for trades.

PART II

The Momentum Oscillators

CHAPTER 4

Relative Strength Index

Overview: Among momentum oscillators, the relative strength index (RSI) is the least complex and easiest to interpret. It sets up an index value between zero and 100 and defines overbought and oversold momentum. Because this is an effective indicator, stocks tend not to remain in these extremes for long, providing an excellent system for timing of reversal and for confirmation of other reversal signals. RSI is useful as a confirming indicator for trend reversal spotted in price; it may also serve as a leading indicator in cases where momentum precedes price reaction. However, RSI may also yield false signals, so it requires confirmation before entering new trades.

An *oscillator* measures the attributes of price movement without tracking direction. For many, this is assumed and accepted, but not fully understood. The oscillator is a measurement of a trend's strength or weakness; it also articulates price behavior in terms of volatility and in how momentum reacts. This distinction between trend and price is widely misunderstood.

A trend is the overall direction in price, which may involve retracements within the trend and short-term trends offsetting the longer-term duration. The trend is most effectively measured and understood by momentum, and relative strength index (RSI) is a thermometer of the trend. In a strong trend, RSI will show no movements into overbought or oversold, or only very brief movements and immediate reversal. This is considered healthy because any moves into overbought or oversold indicate excessive movement of price, or likely conclusion of the current trend.

A price is the day-to-day activity of price, which tends to be chaotic in the short term. However, this short-term chaos can be managed effectively by tracking RSI as the price moves in either direction. Traders should make a distinction between the trend and the price. Price represents the segments of a trend, but it may form an erratic pattern in the short term, with the trend understood in terms of a series of price movements in one direction (upward, downward, or sideways).

In terms of how to employ momentum to identify when price is about to reverse, the tracking of speed and strength in a trend creates reversal indicators that, even while tracking moving averages, also tend to lead price and to anticipate when a trend becomes exhausted. This occurs because the excess movement of the oscillator precedes the reversal in price. As momentum moves into overbought or oversold territory, traders must expect a reversal or retracement, meaning price will move in the opposite direction to correct the violation of the range. This is valuable for day traders and swing traders. The move outside of a middle zone represents a temporary exaggeration of price movement, enabling the trader to time traders to exploit a coming reversal.

Is reversal always immediate? No. A price can remain in overbought or oversold range for many days. However, in most instances, the correction to momentum range will take place very quickly. It is possible to find charts with extended RSI overbought or oversold conditions, but the most likely time is going to be between 1 and 3 days (the perfect timing for a swing trade reversal).

As price moves excessively based on the averages created in momentum oscillators, a signal evolves revealing the likelihood of reversal. RSI is one momentum oscillator that compares average advancing periods and average declining periods over the most recent 14 trading sessions. A balance between these two tends to keep momentum in a midrange because advancing and declining periods usually average out and offset one another. This is a sign of a healthy interaction, the result of buyers and sellers reaching agreement on a price range for the stock. RSI creates an index between zero and 100 and sets up an assumed "normal" index value between 30 and 70. When the index moves above 70, the stock is overbought and when it moves below 30, it is oversold.

This is where confusion sets in. Because a momentum oscillator tracks the rate of change in a trend but not the direction, how can it produce an overbought (bearish) or oversold (bullish) signal? The answer is found in the tracking of price along with the RSI. For the most part, the RSI remains within the 30 to 70 range, and violations above or below tend to be very brief, with the index retracing back into the 30 to 70 range. Many of these violations can be ignored because they accompany price spikes. If the spikes are oddities and price then returns to the established trading range, a move outside of the midrange of RSI will quickly be resolved without any signal of reversal in price. The price strike is likely to quickly retrace, and momentum will do the same.

Employing RSI as an initial signal or as a confirming signal is effective, but it should not be used by itself. Because it is a summary of average advancing and declining sessions, a move above 70 or below 30 is rare and should get your attention. Whether it creates actionable signals is a separate question. The simplicity of RSI, a visual index value created with clearly identified normal ranges, makes it the most popular oscillator. Beyond its simplicity, its reliability for spotting and preceding price reversals makes RSI a powerful predictive signal. However, as with all indicators, it is not 100 percent reliable. False signals are possible and do occur.

The Calculation

To appreciate how to best employ RSI as a trading signal, it is useful to first understand how the index is created. RSI is the sum of the most recent 14 advancing and declining periods. It requires a two-part calculation.

First, the number of periods gaining value and the number losing value are themselves averaged over 14 periods. The average gain is divided by the average loss, to calculate the relative strength (RS) of the 14 days:

$$RS = \text{Average gain} \div \text{Average loss}$$

The averages are updated for each new day, with the oldest session dropped and the newest session added. Average gain is equal to the previous average adjusted for the current gain; and the same adjustment is applied to average loss:

$$\text{Average gain} = (((\text{previous average}) \times 13) + \text{current gain}) \div 14$$
$$\text{Average loss} = (((\text{previous average}) \times 13) + \text{current loss}) \div 14$$

Next, the updated RS (or average gain divided by average loss) is used to arrive at the value of RSI:

$$RSI = 100 - (100 \div (1 + RS))$$

This sets up the index value between zero and 100. Because these averages are continually updated and provide offsetting gain and loss averages, the result is most likely to be an RSI value between 30 and 70; and exceptions are notable because they are temporary and invariably lead to a reversal and movement of price back into the 30 to 70 range.

Because RSI is automatically calculated by the numerous free online charting services, why do you need to know how it is calculated? The answer: Knowing what goes into creation of the momentum oscillator improves your understanding of what it reveals. RSI is limited to analysis of price trends, meaning it reflects an average between rising and falling sessions, with a normal balance between the two and exceptions showing up as moves of the oscillator above 70 or below 30.

Normal Volatility Based on RSI

The "normal" range between 30 and 70 is important in understanding how to incorporate RSI into the analysis of price trends—and more to the point, in identifying when even volatile price behavior remains within normal momentum parameters.

For example, Figure 4.1 provides an example of a volatile price history with clear price- and volume-based reversal signals, but lacking any signals in RSI. In this case, momentum remained in the midrange and did not indicate any instances in which the current price trend was either overbought or oversold.

Two instances were identified in which price jumped. In each case, the signals pointed to increased volatility; however, RSI merely moved within its "normal" range. In the first case, a volume spike and large price jump were accompanied by a long white candlestick. This appeared bullish at first glance. However, two subsequent patterns revealed that the bullish move would not continue. First was the stalling of price between $80 and $81 per share. Second was a lack of signal in RSI. The index moved into the high side of the normal range, but did not provide any exceptional signals.

In the second case, an island cluster (also called island reversal) set up a bearish indicator. The price gaps on both sides of this price pattern created the island, and the decline was confirmed by another volume spike.

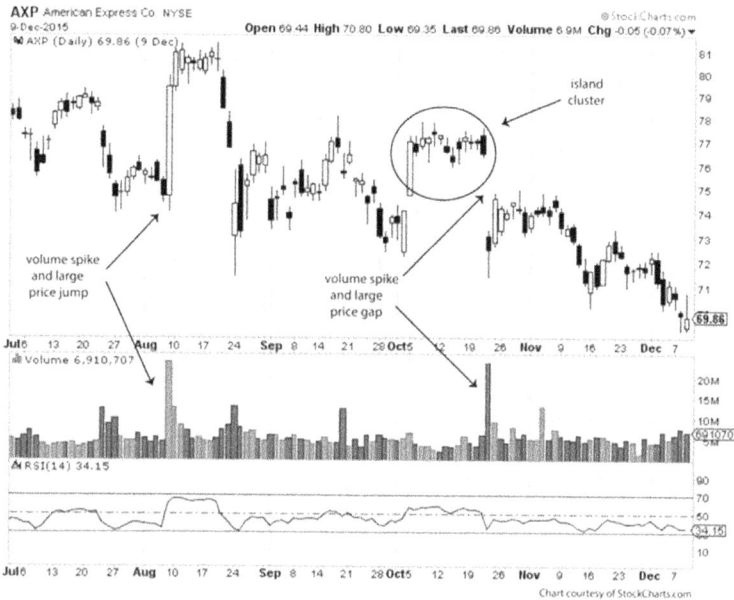

Figure 4.1 Normal RSI levels with volatility

The longer-term bearish trend was further confirmed by RSI remaining in normal range, but only in the area between 30 and 50. This revealed that price activity and volume for the period did not create any significant moves in RSI. However, RSI confirmed the generally bearish trend by not providing any contrary signals.

Does the lack of signals make RSI less useful? No. In fact, the failure of the RSI to move outside of the 30 to 70 range is itself a signal confirming that momentum has not become excessive. Traders must be constantly aware of the possibility that momentum will lead price to levels that are higher or lower than the true supply and demand would normally mandate; and that a reversal could occur just for that reason. When RSI yields no signals, it should be a reassuring signal. In the chart, price volatility was signaled by price and volume indicators; and traders were able to act on those signals. But momentum did not add to what was signaled elsewhere. Based on the RSI's lack of excessive movement, traders were able to rely on price and volume without concern for the possible divergence of momentum.

When divergence does occur, meaning momentum indicates overbought or oversold contrary to what price and volume show, it should not be ignored. Momentum signals usually are more likely to accurately predict a future direction than price or volume, even with strong signals and confirmation.

Overbought Signals

Most traders using RSI look for the exceptional move outside of the normal range. By using RSI as a method for anticipating coming price movement, moves into overbought tend to be very brief, and the index value usually retreats quickly. However, in the chart in Figure 4.2, the RSI remains overbought for 3 weeks. This is rare; however, it should not be ignored. This occurred as part of an exceptionally strong and rapid bullish trend, but RSI reported it as overbought because of the fast price movement. As the conclusion of the chart revealed, RSI correctly predicted a reversal and a downward, offsetting trend.

Part of the initial move into overbought was created by the strong uptrend in October, characterized by a series of small but persistent gaps. In the case of gaps, it is not the size of the gap that matters as much as the recurrence of the pattern. The duration of the overbought condition

Figure 4.2 RSI overbought signal

in RSI is puzzling when this chart is compared to most others; however, it revealed a high likelihood of a price reversal at some point, which often occurs because of recurring gaps in one direction. That point came with a candlestick reversal signal in the form of identical three crows. This is like three black crows, but with each session's closing price identical to the next session's opening price in a downward direction.

The identical three crows is not a common pattern. However, according to one study,[1] a bearish reversal is going to occur in 79 percent of the times that this pattern appears. With the initial reversal provided by RSI, the turning point was marked, and the reversal was confirmed, by this candlestick signal.

This chart gives one example of a strong reversal, partly because of the strong price move after a 3-month consolidation period with resistance holding at $35.25 per share and subsequent move as high as $41 within 1 month. The momentum of this bullish move was likely to go through some degree of adjustment. The big question was when? The combination of unusually long overbought status on RSI and the strong candlestick reversal clearly marked the beginning of a reversing downtrend. The answer is usually found in overbought or oversold levels of momentum. In this unusual case, overbought extended for a lengthy period; and the longer it persisted, the more likely it became that reversal would follow.

Overbought signals are not bearish indicators by themselves. They only reveal that the momentum of the current trend was high. It moved the index into overbought only because the number of advancing periods far exceeded the number of declining periods. However, accompanying that pattern is price. The likely reversal occurs in price as a direct response to momentum in the overbought range.

It is also likely that the strength of a reversal and the duration will be similar or equal to the strength of the previous trend. The longer a trend persists, the more likely the reversal will occur with equal degrees of momentum. In the chart, the reversal that began in early November took price down to nearly the level of the previous resistance price, and this took place over 1 month. The previous bullish move also occurred

---

[1] Bulkowski, T.N. 2012. *Encyclopedia of Candlestick Charts*, 427–35, Vols. 332. Hoboken, NJ: John Wiley & Sons.

over 1 month, marking the likely degree and duration of a reversal, to the previous short-term trend.

Oversold Signals

Like overbought signals, oversold signals identify periods in which the trend has moved rapidly, but with a greater number of declining periods. An interesting example is shown in Figure 4.3.

In this chart, the initial gap was followed by a large black candlestick, a bearish signal. However, two emerging signals strongly pointed to a bullish reversal. The volume spike was not a surprise, based on the trading range of the black candlestick on the same day. The initial move of RSI into oversold territory was also not a great surprise; however, as the price decline flattened out, a reversal became more likely.

The spinning top of August 26 marked the turning point in the downtrend. Another spinning top 2 days earlier, on August 24, is ignored in this analysis, because that was the day of a marketwide large decline. It should be assumed that this affected all price patterns on that date. However, the bottoming out in the downtrend was further marked by

Figure 4.3 RSI oversold signals

the move of RSI out of oversold and back into midrange. RSI remained in midrange for the remainder of the period shown in the chart. These developments clearly marked the conclusion of the downtrend and the beginning of a new uptrend. The return of RSI from oversold to mid-range was a strong signal of coming reversal, confirming the spinning top that first hinted at reversal. Price eventually returned to levels seen before the downtrend, but it took nearly 3 months.

False RSI Signals

If RSI could be revealed as 100 percent reliable, chart analysis would be an easy science. However, any moves to overbought or oversold must be confirmed by other signals, because like most forms of analysis, the momentum oscillator represents a certainty less than 100 percent and acts often as an elusive signal.

For example, in the chart in Figure 4.4, RSI provided two instances of false signals during a generally bullish 6-month period. In both cases, the move above the 70 index value followed a strong uptrend in price, and this is where the uncertainty was born.

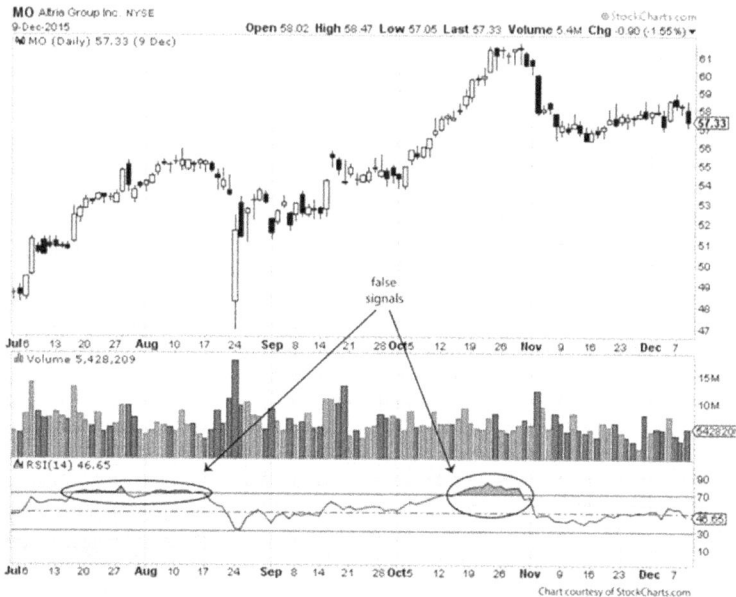

Figure 4.4 RSI false signal

This was a troubling development because RSI remained in over-bought index territory for a longer than average time in both cases. However, the expected bearish reversal did not occur as expected, and the lack of confirmation for any bearish moves revealed that these were both false signals.

The first instance was due to the run-up in price. The big decline on August 24 was due to a marketwide drop, and it took nearly 1 full month for price to regain its previous trading range. The second instance was similar; it resulted from a strong bullish trend lasting 2 weeks. However, once it reached the top, price flattened out and stopped moving. This was a clear sign that the RSI "overbought" status in the last 2 weeks of October would not be likely to lead to a bearish reversal. This condition, the exhaustion of the price trend, is also a signal of exhaustion in momentum for the previous direction—and of a likely reversal to quickly follow. In fact, price declined to take back about half of its previous point growth, only to settle down into a 6-week period of low breadth of trading and very little price movement.

The occurrence of false signals demonstrates that in order to time trades effectively, you need to understand how RSI interacts with other signals, specifically in price and volume. The false signal often follows a strong price move and reflects the lagging effect of averaging, but not a true reversal signal. False signals also tend to occur without any price or volume signal confirmation.

Divergence in RSI

A failed signal is not uncommon in RSI and other oscillators. The reason is basic. Because the oscillator is a summary of price averages, any unusual move in price is likely to cause the index to surge above or below the identified midrange.

Failure is only one version of an indicator without confirmation that goes nowhere. Another is a case of divergence, when the RSI index forecasts a reversal in one direction, but price moves in the opposite direction. During strong trends, divergence is potentially misleading, giving off a false prediction that the trend is about to end and reverse. Like an outright failed signal, divergence must be strongly confirmed before it can be trusted. In these instances, momentum and its predictive value is likely to be more reliable than price or volume, so that divergent momentum should be trusted more than the opposite-trending price or volume.

The issue of failure and divergence is best understood when the calculation of the oscillator is recalled. It represents a smoothing between ascending and descending sessions, and because it is a moving average of price history, it does not always reflect the latest events affecting the price trend. This augments the requirement for independent confirmation. In this chapter, the charts of clear overbought and oversold conditions were accompanied by strong confirming price and volume signals. In the case of the failed RSI signal, there was no confirmation whatsoever. This predicted, accurately in fact, that the move in RSI was not a forecast of strong reversal to follow.

A further method for tracking RSI involves studying the range within the index. The identified midpoint of 50 divides bullish and bearish tendencies. If a bullish market is prevailing, RSI is most likely to show up between 50 and 70 (with overbought moving higher and, possibly, with retracement levels down as low as 40). If a bearish market is prevailing, the RSI range is likely to remain between 50 and 30, with moves below 30 representing oversold, and retracement as high as 60.

These assumptions point out that RSI may easily move into overbought or oversold merely as a reflection of how the price has behaved over the most recent 14 periods, even if future price direction does not follow that development. If the index behaves as it usually does, meaning the move outside of midrange will be brief, there is no need to assume a reversal is in the making. Only when the status remains overbought or oversold for more than a few periods, or when the index spikes into these ranges, is a strong reversal in price likely.

The next chapter expands the discussion of oscillators with an introduction to a more complex one, moving average convergence divergence, or MACD.

Class Questions for Discussion and/or Mini-Case Studies

Multiple Choice

1. RSI identifies overbought or oversold
   (a) strictly as a factor of price accuracy

    (b) based on averaging of price and volume

    (c) based on average of price for the last 14 periods

    (d) favoring strongly bullish markets over bearish markets

2. In observing moves to overbought or oversold

    (a) confirmation is required to validate the signals

    (b) the oscillator is enough by itself to predict coming reversal

    (c) daily volume matters only if it spikes

    (d) price clearly has been distorted by aberrations in the overall market

3. RSI may give off a false signal

    (a) in virtually no cases because it represents a price average

    (b) because of the well-known inefficiency of the market

    (c) because of latest entry in averages and is spotted by lack of confirmation

    (d) when insiders manipulate the stock

4. An RSI divergence consists of

    (a) an oscillator value moving to the extreme, close to 200 or zero

    (b) the oscillator pointing to overbought when the stock is declining, or to oversold when the stock is advancing

    (c) large price gaps as a primary cause

    (d) exceptionally large differences in the price averages advancing and declining

Discussion

Find a chart demonstrating the following: overbought conditions, confirmation, and a subsequent price move to the upside; oversold conditions, confirmation, and a subsequent price move to the downside; a case of RSI briefly moving above 70 or below 30 without confirmation.

CHAPTER 5

Moving Average Convergence Divergence

Overview: The oscillator moving average convergence divergence (MACD) is complex in comparison to other oscillators. It consists of three moving averages (MAs) interacting with one another and is focused on the significance of MA crossover. As a means for confirmation of other signals, MACD may be used as one of several oscillators to identify trends as they strengthen or weaken. However, the frequent crossover occurrence may also mislead analysts; MACD, consequently, is appropriate for confirmation of other signals, but rarely can be applied as an initial reversal signal.

The momentum oscillator moving average convergence divergence (MACD) consists of three separate moving averages (MAs). The visual interaction between the three provides signals for bullish or bearish trending. However, the most valuable—and most ignored—advantage to MACD is found in a divergence strategy.

MACD follows trends by demonstrating the endless association of one average to another. Just as the simpler MA flags crossover, MACD is a more sophisticated version of the same idea. Its two primary averages are 26-day and 12-day and rather than performing as simple MAs, both are exponential moving averages (EMAs). The calculation of EMA builds greater weight in the most recent entry to the field of sessions, so that current information influences movement more than older information.

The limited time involved (26 and 12 days) minimizes the impact of this weighting in the averages; however, EMA makes sense statistically, based on the tendency for price information to quickly become outdated and replaced by more relevant developments. Even 26 or 12 days may constitute a lengthy period in market analysis, even though the statistical value of such short periods is dubious.

In the MACD calculation, the longer (26-day) EMA is subtracted from the shorter (12-day) EMA to identify what is termed the MACD line. In addition to these averages, a third EMA of 9 days, termed the signal line, is overlaid on the other two averages, and this is where proponents of MACD claim trading signals occur. When the initial two averages cross above the signal line, it is considered a buy signal; and when the two signals cross below the signal line, it represents a sell signal.

Beyond crossover, divergence may also play a role in chart analysis. In this application of the oscillator, when the MACD signal is divergent from price or volume signals, the momentum is most likely to prevail and produce reliable signals. Traders relying on momentum and divergence from price often find that the predictive value of that divergence is worth paying attention to and acting upon—assuming that independent confirmation of the divergence is located as well.

In this strategy, both the oscillator and the price are tracked, a technique that should always apply to momentum analysis. With MACD, the strongest forms of divergence can point to improved trade timing. A bullish divergence is mostly likely to be found during an uptrend and once price moves downward into an oversold region. Combining not two but three indicators will create an effective use of oscillators:

1. Identify the prevailing trend. For example, as prices rise, the trend clearly is bullish, notably when price rises above resistance.
2. Track relative strength index (RSI) and look for instances when the oscillator moves below the 30 index value into oversold territory, or above 70 into overbought.
3. Finally, look to MACD to discover whether you find confirmation or divergence. When price moves below support or above resistance and RSI signals overbought or oversold, confirmation or divergence may be observed in MACD.

Understanding MACD

Traders need to understand what MACD consists of—three separate MAs. These consist of a 12-day EMA, a 26-day EMA, and a 9-day EMA. There are three specific segments to the MACD visual. The MACD line is the net of the 12-day minus the 26-day. The signal line is the 9-day

EMA. And finally, the centerline consists of the MACD line minus the signal line.

Even though traders generally understand this interaction, the significance of the combined set of outcomes is not well understood. Most traders focus on signal crossover to identify bullish or bearish reversals. The problem with this application of MACD is found in the fact that MAs are always lagging indicators. Crossover is frequent and produces numerous false signals. The complexity of interaction among the various lines of MACD makes it a special oscillator, one with less reliability than other ones but of exceptional value when studied for divergence signals.

The lagging nature of all MAs is a problem. In the case of MACD, all of the MAs are of extremely short duration, so that a two-part problem emerges. First, the value of identified crossover is in doubt. Second, the lagging nature of the oscillator points to the need for independent confirmation; and with the likelihood of frequent false signals, this is not always possible. Or, even when confirmation is discovered, it is often too late to act in advance of the anticipated price move.

Once a reversal has been spotted, it may be too late to enter a timely trade. However, if you have relied on other reversals to time your trades, an MACD crossover is one form of confirmation; however, caution is in order due to the uncertainty of this indicator, so other signals are also necessary prior to entering a trade. The added confirmation provided by MACD is probably the extent of value to crossover analysis. In comparison, a divergence strategy tends to occur at the same time as a price trend and, despite the reliance on MAs, may even provide a leading indicator of what comes next.

The term "divergence" is confusing as well, because it has two distinct and different meanings. For most analysts relying on oscillators, divergence is the opposite of convergence. As two MAs move toward one another, it is "convergence." And as these lines begin to move apart, it is "divergence." The 12-day MA is faster than the 26-day, and as a result tends to react to price movement more rapidly. This is what causes convergence and divergence under this definition. MACD produces numerous minor crossover signals, but their value cannot be determined until it is demonstrated that the crossover is not incidental. By the time the crossover is established as part of a price trend, it is too late to act.

Even so, many traders assign great value to MACD crossover. The centerline is unchanging, and the MACD line moves either above or below. This is where crossover occurs and where most traders make use of MACD. Once both signals cross above the fixed centerline (bullish) or below that line (bearish), the signal is recognized. Another application of these MA trends is a belief that when the shorter-term (12-day) EMA moves higher than the 26-day and is above it, the bullish signal increases; and when the direction is lower, the bearish signal increases. However, this normal application of MACD ignores the more advantageous use of the oscillator to spot a different form of divergence: directional differences between price and momentum.

Divergence of a Different Type

Centerline crossover is the most popular use of MACD, where the oscillator is used in the same manner as other oscillators. However, in any case where reliance is on lagging indicators, the value is dubious, notably with the use of extremely short-term averages. In that case, the volatility of short-term changes may easily mislead a trader to rely on signals that reflect not actual momentum, but short-term uncertainty and volatility.

If a signal appears after reversal has occurred, what value is it? In comparison, a divergence strategy based on trending in opposite direction between oscillator and price provides a more powerful version of "divergence." When the timing of analysis is based on RSI overbought or oversold movement, the transition to MACD to check for divergence is a wise timing strategy. It adds strength to what is revealed in the analysis of MACD divergence, versus the less reliable crossover study.

The form of divergence giving out value and reliability is found when the direction of the MA lines is opposite to the price trend. This version of "MACD divergence" is not like the typical lagging indicator based on combined MA analysis. A bullish divergence occurs when the stock price hits a lower low and the MACD direction moves to a higher low. For example, Figure 5.1 provides an example of two instances in which price was on the decline while MACD was rising. This bullish divergence demonstrated that the bearish price trend would not hold.

The initial steep downtrend occurred even while MACD was trending upward; although remaining below the centerline, the direction of

Figure 5.1 Bullish divergence

movement is what created divergence. The end of the downtrend was anticipated by MACD, even though it was not clearly marked until a combination of three signals: the long lower shadow, volume spike, and oversold signal in RSI. MACD's divergence occurred in advance of the price reversal. This confirms what the other three signals anticipated.

After a brief divergence in the opposite direction, MACD resumed an upward trend during the month of September, while prices once again trended downward. As RSI briefly touched the 30 index marking the oversold condition, the price saw a reversal day in the long white shadow, then a gap, and strong rebound. MACD divergence anticipated the turn from bearish to bullish.

The same level of divergence anticipating price direction in advance of price occurs when forecasting a bearish reversal. For example, Figure 5.2 shows a case of divergence that starts with the RSI rising to the 70 level, the point where the price is overbought. Preceding this were two volume spikes. The MACD decline began in early November, even though the price level was flattening out but showing no signs of reversal.

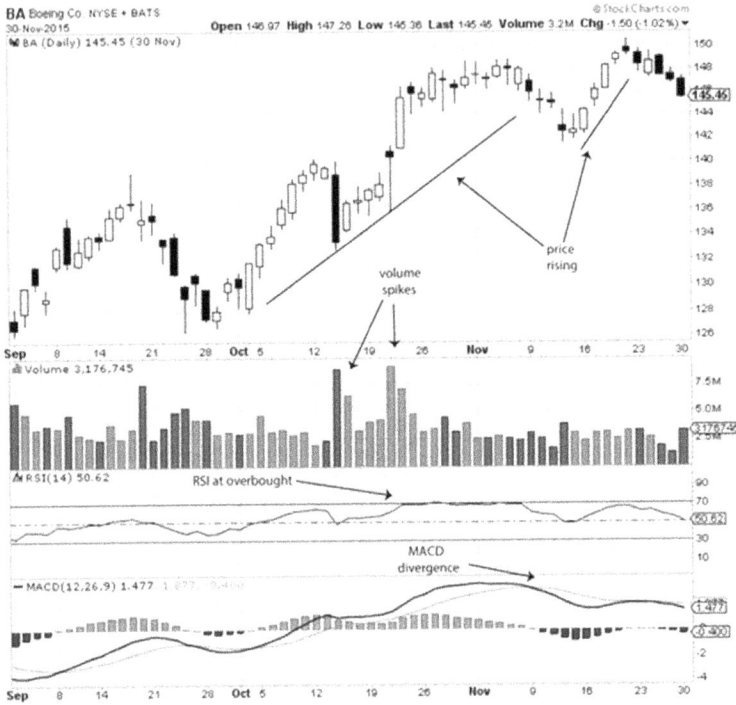

Figure 5.2 Bearish divergence

In this formation, the combination of all these signals (RSI, volume, and MACD) indicated that reversal was about to occur. The strength of the price move was contradicted by both RSI and MACD. The strong divergence shown in MACD should be given greater importance than the price trend in this case.

Figure 5.3 reveals what happened next. As forecast previously, price turned downward sharply. There had been no price-based signals of reversal, and that also is a key. When reversal signals are not apparent, look for divergence in MACD and other oscillators. The forecast occurred only in the combined momentum and volume warnings.

This analysis reveals the type of divergence-based analysis that is necessary when price does not provide initial reversal signals, or when reversal is not strongly confirmed with other signals. In these examples, MACD led the way by making a directional move before price. The lagging indicator of price averages became the leading indicator of reversal, occurring well in advance of the price reversal. Why did this happen? The move in

Figure 5.3 Bearish divergence and results

MACD reflected a weakening in the MAs, the change anticipating the reversal in momentum leading to a reversal in price. This change was not visible, however, in price by itself. It is the combined series of MAs, calculated using the MACD formula, that are expressed by divergence.

Emphasis is usually put on the other type of divergence, separation between the 12-day and 26-day averages. This provides value, notably as the two averages both cross over the centerline. However, the real value is found in reversal signals because MAs by themselves are lagging indicators; and the shorter-term average is expected to be more responsive to price movement than the longer-term average. Assigning value to divergence between the two MA lines is a self-fulfilling prophecy, with significance occurring after the price move itself. This develops with timing, making the signal ineffective; it will be too late to act once the signal has been recognized.

If analysis of MACD is limited to crossover of the averages, it is of little use in analysis. Because the signals are short term and complex, they should be expected to express the volatility associated with short-term price behavior. A study of most charts, notably those with volatile price activity, reveals that MACD crossover occurs frequently and often has no predictive value. However, when MACD diverges from price, traders should pay attention. This often signals a coming reversal, recognized in MACD divergence in advance of changes in price direction.

Divergence between momentum and price is far more meaningful than crossover between the short-term MACD averages, especially when the divergence is confirmed by volume spikes or by other volume-based reversal signals. These signals include on-balance volume, accumulation/distribution, the Chaikin oscillator, Chaikin money flow, and the money flow index. These are beyond the scope of this discussion. However, volume spikes and other indicators should not be ignored; they provide confirmation, both of price reversal and MACD divergence signals. One of the observations in technical analysis (notably in the Dow theory) is that volume precedes price, meaning that movement in volume indicators should be expected to represent a first signal that price is about to reverse. However, volume by itself is not always a reliable metric for what occurs in price. Many things influence volume, notably the activity of institutional investors. Institutions control the majority of trades in the market, so decisions by mutual fund managers, pension plan, or insurance companies may create higher than average volume, but may also occur in isolation from more significant market events, notably those based on management activity, earnings reports, or perceptions of future value in a company's stock based on analysts' changing recommendations (e.g., buy to hold or sell).

The use of volume along with momentum adds greater value; and divergence is perhaps the best use of MACD, which when confirmed by changes in volume, aids in the timing of trades based on anticipated reversal.

The unique feature of MACD compared with other oscillators is the combined reporting of momentum and trend together. For many traders, this combination adds value to what otherwise would be restricted to price analysis. However, as a statistical principle, short-term averages tend to be less reliable than long-term averages. The combined use of short-term averages means that MACD often represents the expected volatility of price in the short term, and this detracts from the understanding of momentum as a means for anticipating price reversal.

MACD, as a result, is not reliable for identifying overbought or oversold conditions. For that, other oscillators, notably RSI, are stronger and more reliable. The reliance of MACD on short-term price behavior can be translated to describe how price affects the outcome: The greater the price volatility over the term of the EMAs, the more distortion should be expected. This is especially the case when the most recent prices are volatile, because exponential averaging gives greater weight to the most recent values.

The next chapter presents another centered oscillator, rate of change. It is like MACD in many respects but is a simplified version of momentum measurement.

Class Questions for Discussion and/or Mini-Case Studies

Multiple Choice

1. MACD is a complex oscillator, consisting of
   (a) both an EMA and simple MA
   (b) three simple MAs of 12, 26, and 9 sessions
   (c) combined price and volume averages
   (d) three EMAs of 12, 26, and 9 sessions
2. MACD works well with price and
   (a) confirms overbought or oversold moves in RSI
   (b) anticipates volume spikes and price gaps
   (c) tracks price movement closely, providing dynamic resistance and support
   (d) supersedes the value of other oscillators that are not as reliable
3. The true value in MACD is found in
   (a) crossover of the averages, confirming price reversal
   (b) divergence from what is observed in price and RSI
   (c) convergence of dissimilar lines as a leading indicator
   (d) convergence of the centerline with price

Mini-Case Study

Referring to Figures 5.2, analyze what took place in the extended period shown in Figure 5.3. First, check price and RSI to discover reversal signals and confirmation. Next, add in the divergence of MACD and explain why this strongly indicates that the longer-term price direction is misleading when divergence is not studied.

CHAPTER 6

Rate of Change

Overview: The rate of change (ROC) oscillator is an alternative measurement of momentum, setting up a centerline as a "zero" value, with movement either above or below, each indicating varying degrees of momentum. A major drawback is the lack of limitation on movement away from the zero line; however, ROC does not measure averages, but does quantify changes in price over a set period and, as a result, changes in momentum.

Rate of change (ROC) is a centered oscillator, meaning the middle line value is treated as an index with a value of zero. The ROC line moves above or below this level and provides specific types of momentum signals.

ROC compares the current price of stock to the 12 periods immediately preceding the day. This forms the ROC oscillator. The most obvious outcome of this calculation is obvious: The higher the volatility of a single day and the lower the volatility of the previous 12 days, the more movement ROC will report. The 12-day change (current day less the price 12 days earlier) can vary considerably based on changes in price volatility. The opposite also applies. If past price movement has been exceptionally volatile, but it settles down in the current period, ROC momentum will appear to be low. Overall, because ROC is a relative measurement, it must be viewed along with other indicators and never alone. The most useful application of ROC is not to measure current momentum, but to find and react to divergence. If the momentum signal from ROC moves opposite the direction of price, it could anticipate a coming reversal.

However, ROC is different than other oscillators because it is not as reliable in forecasting reversal because of divergence. This is due to the method of calculation. The apparent divergence often results from changes in volatility during the short term of analysis for ROC, rather than pegged to actual overbought or oversold conditions.

The default measurement is a 12-day change in price, but this can be adjusted to increase or decrease momentum responsiveness to price changes. The longer the period is, the lower the change will be and the fewer signals generated; for example, some analysts prefer a 20-day period. However, this longer period is often difficult to interpret due to the potential to miss important ROC signals. The default can also be reduced, but this increases signals and adds to the potential for false signals.

ROC is difficult to interpret due to the limitless extent the signal can move either above or below the line. Does a higher or lower move in ROC equate to stronger momentum? No, because the significance of ROC movement is relative to previous levels and degrees of change. This means that as ROC moves, it must be understood in relation to previous movements in the index. For this reason and due to the confusion resulting from the behavior of the oscillator, ROC is not as popular as relative strength index (RSI) or moving average convergence divergence (MACD). Its signals are not always clear. Like MACD, the ROC oscillator has value when it points to divergence or when these other momentum signals are not clear; and as a divergence measure, it can be used to confirm or contradict reversal signals found elsewhere.

Why is ROC unbounded in the degree it may change? This is the format because the value can in theory expand without limitation, even in a short timeframe. A rising ROC points to likely bullish movement, and a declining ROC to bearish movement. However, these general observations can be misleading if the beginning or ending prices are not typical of the current trend. Oscillators are intended to measure overbought and oversold conditions and not necessarily to identify bullish and bearish conditions. Because ROC is strictly limited to price and its short-term trends, its overbought and oversold status is also relative and cannot be called a true momentum measurement.

This limitation is seen when price volatility declines. As price consolidates and moves sideways, ROC is expected to remain close to the zero line. However, due to the calculation of ROC, overbought and oversold are relative values. The ROC index could continue fluctuating because past volatility is included in the period of 12 days. Consequently, ROC acts often as a deferred measurement, a true lagging indicator. This can produce deceptive and false signals. In comparison, in RSI, the extent of gains and losses is considered, so overbought and oversold levels are rarely seen and when they appear, they tend to last only a short time. ROC is in a sense a victim of the daily movement in price rather than a calculation of average gains versus average losses.

The Calculation

ROC simply measures the degree of net change in price. This makes it one of the easiest oscillators to understand, but its value relies on price volatility and extent of trend movement within the period. Another flaw in ROC is that a change in the trend direction during the period could result in what appears to be low volatility, even when interim price movement was active. As price reverses, the difference from the beginning to the end of the period under study will also be smoothed, perhaps artificially.

This problem is apparent in a review of the ROC calculation:

$$((c - c^n) - c^n) \times 100 = \text{ROC}$$

In this calculation c represents the latest session's closing price and c^n represents the closing price 12 sessions earlier. Consequently, if either of these values is untypical of what has occurred in the interim sessions, ROC will not be reliable. Likewise, if interim sessions have spiked above or below the "typical" price behavior reflected in the values of c and c^n at any point, the volatility will not be reflected in the outcome. These drawbacks demonstrate that ROC is not completely reliable for measuring true momentum. In the trend of price, momentum should take volatility into account to truly reflect how price is moving and to judge where that might move in coming sessions.

ROC is not an analysis of moving averages, but only of the net change in price from the beginning to the end of the period. Herein lies the flaw of ROC: Volatility might not be reflected at all for a single ROC entry, and overbought or oversold conditions might be in effect in the moment but not as part of a trend or of changes in momentum. This applies whether price moved either upward or downward over the period in question; the net ROC might be low even as momentum was high. The change from beginning to end of the period would not reflect interim volatility; and on a chart, ROC is likely to track price movement accurately; thus, the true measure of momentum is not as reliable as in oscillators based on moving averages. However, the value of ROC is found in the longer-term trend it provides as a form of divergence opposite price-based signals.

The recognition of a bullish or bearish ROC is self-fulfilling, because the calculation is merely that of the percentage of change in price and not on a trend or of actual price momentum. The ROC is a momentum oscillator because it involves multiple periods, but its true value is as an additional source of information when other momentum tests do not give out strong indicators. The value in ROC is twofold: as confirmation of the current price trend despite volatility and as a divergence signal forecasting coming price reversals.

Utilizing ROC Effectively

The first use of ROC is for confirmation. It can serve as one of many signals to be used in addition to other signals—price, volume, and momentum—forecasting reversal. The chart in Figure 6.1 provides an example of how this works.

In this example, two periods of consolidation were separated by a flip from prior support to new resistance. This is a commonly seen phenomenon in stock charts, but it does not always mean a flip in direction. In this case, for example, the trading range shifted but replaced one five-point trading range with a lower four-point trading range, two consolidation trends. Most noteworthy on this chart is that the two highlighted ROC periods occurred in advance of the predicted price behavior. This is notable because at the same time, RSI produces no signals of overbought or oversold.

For many traders and investors, making any decisions during consolidation is both frustrating and confusing. Traders tend to avoid trading at all until a new bullish or bearish trend takes over. However, using momentum with price and volume signals allows identification of clear price trend signals. In this case, volume spikes accompanied failed breakouts, in both cases below support level. Recognizing this pattern allows for timely swing trades, anticipating a likely move back into range. This reliable pattern is strengthened when short-term price movement is identified with momentum as well.

Figure 6.1 ROC as confirmation of price trend

For the RSI faithful, this is a frustrating chart. RSI remained within the 30 to 70 midrange index for the entire period, when a view of the chart would indicate strong movement outside of consolidation. Price was volatile, but RSI did not reflect that volatility. However, in both strong downward moves, ROC acted as a leading indicator. Beginning in mid-October when price was trying to break through resistance at the top of the range, ROC began a sharp decline—in advance of the strong price move below support in the second half of the month. Again, in mid-November, ROC anticipated a price decline below support, which set up the new, lower trading range. Once the new range was established, ROC's volatility settled down to lower levels.

This chart shows the failure of RSI to add any momentum-based intelligence concerning price movement, but ROC was a strong substitute that took over as a leading indicator and as confirmation for the volume spikes occurring in each breakout below support. However, for traders relying on momentum to signal reversal, how is the decision made to rely on RSI or ROC? This is a difficult question because in many instances, ROC is erratic whereas RSI accurately measures overbought and oversold conditions and yields strong and predictive signals. In the chart in Figure 6.1, only about eight points were involved from top to bottom. This means that RSI is less likely to produce signals due to the low point spread. In comparison, ROC is more likely to act as a leading indicator; it measures change from the beginning to the end of the period, regardless of the point spread involved. In charts with a great point spread, RSI is more likely to produce reliable signals, and ROC is more vulnerable to distortion due to a greater percentage of change from one period to another.

ROC as a Divergence Signal

Another value in ROC is its use for divergence signaling. The chart of Alleghany (Y) makes this point, as shown in Figure 6.2.

Figure 6.2 ROC divergence signals

This chart was difficult to read until mid-October, when an exceptionally long upper shadow forecast buying weakness. Buyers were not able to move prices higher, and this anticipated the decline that started nearly 2 months later. A similar forecast was identified in early September when the unusually long lower shadow revealed weakness on the sell side. The long lower shadow was a sign of weakening sell sentiment. The October upper shadow provided a similar indication that buying sentiment was weakening.

Reading a single upper shadow is not an easy task without confirmation, and despite this event in mid-October, prices continued edging upward. However, near the end of the month, RSI briefly moved above the 70 index value for the first (and only) time on the chart. By itself, this very brief movement in RSI was not especially meaningful. However, it marked the beginning of a 6-week decline in ROC, representing divergence from price. As the price level trended up as high as $515 per share, ROC began a decline from bullish range down below the zero line and into the bearish side. This ROC trend preceded price reversal of early December and accurately predicted a correction of 55 points in the following 6 weeks. This was an example of ROC acting as a divergent signal and as a leading indicator.

Any investor or trader relying on single indicators of any kind is taking a chance, and this applies to ROC as well as to any other indicator. However, this exercise demonstrates that ROC, like MACD, is effective as either a substitute for RSI or a signal of divergence, like the best use of MACD.

The problems of ROC based on how it is calculated must be kept in mind in this analysis. However, the point should not be ignored: On some charts, ROC sets up divergence and leads price. But it should be understood in terms of what caused the divergent price. Since the beginning of October, price began a strong bullish move. This showed down by the middle of the month, so the 12-day analysis of beginning and ending price also was reduced. From that point to the end of the first week in December, the net change in all 12-day periods declined. This declining momentum was a signal of divergence, but it was not enough by itself to generate a bearish trade. The single RSI overbought signal was so brief that it also provided limited value. However, during this period, numerous candlestick reversal signals were found, confirming that ROC predicted a bearish reversal.

Applying ROC to Identify Extreme Levels

The most valuable application for ROC is as confirmation for volume and price signals. However, when price levels rise or fall to the extreme, one place this is most easily identified is in momentum. RSI is the most reliable oscillator for identifying overbought or oversold conditions in cases of extreme price movement, but because it relies on price change from the beginning to the end of only 12 days, by the time this shows up, it might be too late to act upon the information. In this form of momentum, it truly is a lagging indicator, good for confirmation but often appearing too late to act.

ROC is not based on moving averages but on the percentage of change in price levels between two sessions 12 days apart. The smoothing tendency of momentum oscillators based on moving averages contains a flaw but the flaw in ROC is that it compares two prices and bases the calculation of these without consideration for what occurs in between. In dynamic trends (bullish or bearish), ROC tends to track the trend and to adjust for retracements at the same time as price. In consolidation trends, ROC will act in a similar manner, moving sideways with price. However, ROC is not especially useful in spotting breakouts above or below consolidation. The exception to this is when ROC is used to confirm what shows up as possible breakout patterns in price and volume (especially volume spikes). It also adds to analytical ability to spot or anticipate price reversal through momentum divergence.

Taking this a step beyond, the degree of change in ROC away from the zero line can be significant as well. Most observations of ROC reveal a simple formulation: Above the zero line is a bullish signal, and below is a bearish signal. However, as shown in both preceding examples, ROC tends to move farther away from that zero line when price is also spiking higher or lower. Because this tends to occur at the same time, the significance of changes in ROC is limited. However, it does provide another piece in the puzzle of analysis and the attempt to anticipate and forecast price movement.

The next chapter studies another piece in the momentum puzzle, the stochastic oscillator. This is another form of momentum testing that is often overlooked or poorly understood. However, it provides you with analytical confirmation of changes in momentum.

Class Questions for Discussion and/or Mini-Case Studies

Multiple Choice

1. ROC measures
   (a) changes in the slope of a trend over time
   (b) speed of the changes in price
   (c) changes in price from the beginning to the end of a period
   (d) degree of overbought and oversold
2. A flaw in ROC is that
   (a) interim volatility is not highlighted
   (b) price itself is not part of the equation
   (c) the calculation is overly complex
   (d) there are too many moving average measurements to interpret
3. ROC works best when
   (a) used as a stand-alone indicator
   (b) the stock price is highly volatile
   (c) no other oscillators are available
   (d) RSI does not provide reliable or actionable signals

True or False

1. ROC is useful as a signal of divergence.
2. ROC measures pure momentum.
3. The purpose behind ROC is restricted to initial forecasting.

Discussion

Locate a chart revealing a price trend with confirmation by RSI, but when ROC is in divergence. Demonstrate how the divergence of ROC worked to not only contradict when price and RSI predicted, but ended up correctly identifying an unexpected reversal.

CHAPTER 7

The Stochastic Oscillator

Overview: The stochastic oscillator is like relative strength index (RSI) in the sense that it sets up an index valued between zero and 100. However, it employs two moving averages and identifies overbought above 80 and oversold below 20. As an alternative, it adds value to momentum tracking when used in conjunction with RSI, or for confirmation of other oscillators and indicators.

Among oscillators, the stochastic may be the most obscure. The word "stochastic" is a statistical term meaning *random probability*, which at first glance is not especially reassuring to the analyst on an unending quest for predictability. However, despite its odd name, the stochastic oscillator adds an element of confirmation to what price trends appear to predict.

Comparison to RSI

Although relative strength index (RSI) and stochastic oscillators perform a similar service, there are differences. Both identify overbought and oversold (70 to 30 for RSI and 80 to 20 for stochastic). The strongest method for use of stochastic is alongside RSI. This helps provide momentum confirmation between the two oscillators or may also point to divergence.

RSI tracks price movement to articulate the degree of momentum in the current trend. Stochastic is different in how it works. It assumes that price should close in conformity with the current trend, and if price varies from this, it could be the first signal that the trend is concluding. This difference seems subtle at first, but it means that RSI provides the greatest value during trending markets and stochastic is more insightful when price behavior is inconsistent and volatile. For example, a strong trend is difficult to follow because traders need to understand when the trend is slowing down or about to reverse. It is often the case that a move into overbought (during a bullish trend) or oversold (in a bearish trend) is the first sign of coming reversal, predicting price to soon respond. Stochastic is more useful in managing wide swings in price and bringing some order to short-term price chaos.

However, stochastic comes with limitations as well as with benefits. The oscillator tends to provide many false signals, often the consequence of short-term volatility and the uncertainty about whether a strong trend can develop at such times. The false signals associated with the stochastic oscillator occur often; for this reason, stochastic is not reliable alone but may work as a confirmation or divergent indicator.

It is based on comparison between a current closing price and a range of prices over the last 14 consecutive sessions. The oscillator establishes an index between zero and 100, with overbought above 80 and oversold below 20. The two lines developed in stochastic are signals of the value of this oscillator for each session, and a 3-day average of the first line. A 3-day average is exceptionally short term, and the statistical limitations of such a brief average should be kept in mind when determining the value of the momentum oscillator. The purpose of the double lines is based on the theory that price responds to momentum, so when the two lines converge, it is a signal of coming reversal. Divergence also points to possible reversal. When a trend reaches a new high or low, but the stochastic moves in a direction opposite to price, it may be taken as anticipation of reversal.

More precisely, stochastic does not measure momentum directly, but is meant to measure degrees of momentum in price movement. Thinking of stochastic as a test of the level of momentum may point to greater value than simply as a test of overbought or oversold, as seen in RSI and other oscillators.

Because both convergence and divergence are thought to signal coming reversal, the stochastic oscillator must be viewed with caution. Therefore, stochastic and RSI, when studied together, provide more reliable confirmation than stochastic alone.

The Oscillator and How It Works

The stochastic oscillator is a combination of two moving averages involving three different prices: high, low, and closing. The calculation is performed over 14 periods. The randomness in the name of this oscillator refers to a combination of two separate calculations to create the index value. However, these are directly related, as the combination reveals a price trend in terms not of closing price, but of daily breadth of trading, and sets up a view of momentum expressed by price movement.

Like RSI, the oscillator in this case sets up a value between zero and 100, with the index value at or above 80 identifying "overbought" and at or below 20 as "oversold." The difference, however, is in the use of the high, low, and closing prices, versus RSI's employment of closing prices only. This means that stochastic takes daily breadth of trading and volatility into account, so that it acts more like a leading indicator than RSI and, as a result, may also provide more timely forecasts of reversal in the price trend, even with its tendency to create false signals, especially during times of highly volatile and erratic price movement.

Analysts have noted that prices tend to close at or near the highest or lowest points in the trading range immediately before reversal. Another way of expressing this is in reference to proximity. Reversal signals tend to be strongest when they appear near resistance (bearish reversal) or support (bullish reversal). In comparison, reversal signals appearing at the middle of an established range tend to be weaker and less reliable; the signal may not materialize, or it could reflect coincidental price behavior rather than a signal. The stochastic oscillator is a reliable form of confirmation for reversal signals in other forms (price, volume, moving average, and other oscillators), or when proximity is perfect (signals found at the point of resistance or support, or gapping through those levels), even as a leading indicator itself. However, in all cases, the stochastic reversal signal must be confirmed by other signals before it is considered wise to enter a trade.

Considering that stochastic tends to issue false signals too often to make it a reliable forecaster of reversal, a study of resistance and support is useful in confirming reversal signals stochastic generates. Traditional resistance and support consist of straight lines above and below the current price range; these may move sideways or diagonally and tend to be strongest when the breadth of trading remains the same until it expands. This is the point where reversal is likely to begin. However, the straight lines of resistance and support are inflexible and may not always identify coming reversal. An alternative is to overlay Bollinger Bands over price, and to consider the two standard deviations between upper and lower bands as dynamic levels of resistance or support.

This provides a stronger version of trading breadth and borders. However, violations above the upper band or below the lower band are rare. An adjustment may be to define the trading range of a bullish move between upper band and middle band and of a bearish move between middle and lower bands. When this version of the trading range is observed, the signals in stochastic are strengthened and, if confirmed with other signals, become more effective in anticipating coming reversal.

The Calculation

The calculation of the stochastic oscillator begins with a 14-day calculation known as %K. The formula for %K is

$$100[(cc - lc) \div (hh - ll)] = \%K$$

where cc is the current closing price, lc the lowest close during 14 periods, hh the highest high during 14 periods, and ll the lowest low during 14 periods.

The difference between the current closing price and the lowest price during the last 14 sessions, divided by the difference between the highest high and the lowest low during the period, yields the %K value of the latest session as the close.

The second calculation is known as %D and consists of the average of the three most recent %K results:

$$[\%K_3 + \%K_2 + \%K_1] \div 3 = \%D$$

These calculations create a two-line stochastic result, one each for %K and %D. Unlike RSI with its single line index, stochastic contains two lines, which adds a dimension to the identification of overbought or oversold and, as a result, to bullish or bearish signals. A strong bullish indication is given when %D and %K both move below the index 20 (oversold); or a bearish indication when both move above the index 80 (overbought). Some analysts contend that divergence between the two signals adds additional bullish signaling, but this is not as reliable as tracking of both averages below 20 or above 80.

In these extremes, above 80 or below 20, another attribute should be noted. At the levels above 80 or below 20, periods of accumulation or distribution are identified. This concept (accumulation/distribution, A/D) is based solely on volume, so that stochastic extremes may confirm what the A/D line reveals at the same time—combining momentum with volume as a *leading* indicator. The Dow theory is based in part on the idea that volume leads price, so when stochastic confirms the volume-based A/D indicator, the signal is confirmed.

A/D identifies buying and selling pressure based on volume. However, volume may increase unexpectedly and for a variety of causes. These causes can include anticipation of earnings surprises, impending ex-dividend date, or rumors concerning mergers and acquisitions, changes in management, and other elements affecting volume alone or volume and price. For these reasons, confirming A/D with stochastic is one way to gain confirmation in a confusing or volatile time. When the stochastic averages move below 20, it may also confirm a similar bullish signal in A/D, or above 80 confirm a bearish signal in A/D.

A/D in Conjunction with Stochastic

The A/D is a volume indicator that studies the money flow in and out of a stock. It is cumulative, so that the analysis over a period of moving averages is what develops this signal. A/D is used as confirmation of price or momentum or of both.

A/D is calculated in three steps:

1. Money flow multiplier (MFM):
   [(close − low) − (high − close)] ÷ (high − low) = MFM
2. Money flow volume (MFV):
   MFM × Volume for the period = MFV
3. A/D line:
   Previous A/D line + Current MFV = A/D line

A/D varies between +1 and −1. It is positive when a session's close is in the upper portion of the high to low range; and it is negative when the close is in the lower portion. As a cumulative measurement of volume flow, high volume and A/D are an indication of bullish pressure, and low volume and A/D are the opposite, a bearish indication.

Although A/D itself can be used to signal a bullish or bearish reversal or continuation, it may also be used along with the stochastic oscillator to confirm likely reversal soon. Divergence plays a strong role in the A/D line. This is seen when A/D indicates sentiment in one direction, but price moves in the opposite direction. This would be confusing if limited to A/D and price. However, when divergence is combined with the analysis of stochastic (or a combination of stochastic and RSI), it adds a secondary layer of confirmation. This is an example of how volume confirms price, but more significantly, how it also confirms momentum signals.

Stochastic as Confirmation

Although stochastic signals may serve as leading indicators of price reversal, a trader should be reluctant to place too much reliance on this idea. The Russian proverb *doveryay, no proveryay* (trust but verify) should rule the use of stochastic. It is an effective form of confirmation as well and may be more reliable when used in this context. Like RSI, stochastic is based on moving averages. Although stochastic is different from RSI, the same caution applies. However, it often occurs that strong price reversal cannot be confirmed by RSI, but stochastic works well in this role as an alternative.

This occurs because the use of 14 periods in both oscillators may yield significantly different signals. RSI is likely to remain in midrange over an extended period with only occasional forays above 80 or below 20, or with no movement outside of midrange at all. At the same time, stochastic is likely to yield valuable and strong signals at a higher frequency. This observation is based on the extremes of both %K and %D moving outside of the midrange index. The subtle interaction between the two averages can be discounted because, in most cases, the two lines track close to one another. Movement of one above or below the other often is so slight that no specific signal can be taken reliably.

An example of the differences between RSI and stochastic, and of how stochastic is a reliable source for reversal confirmation, is shown in Figure 7.1.

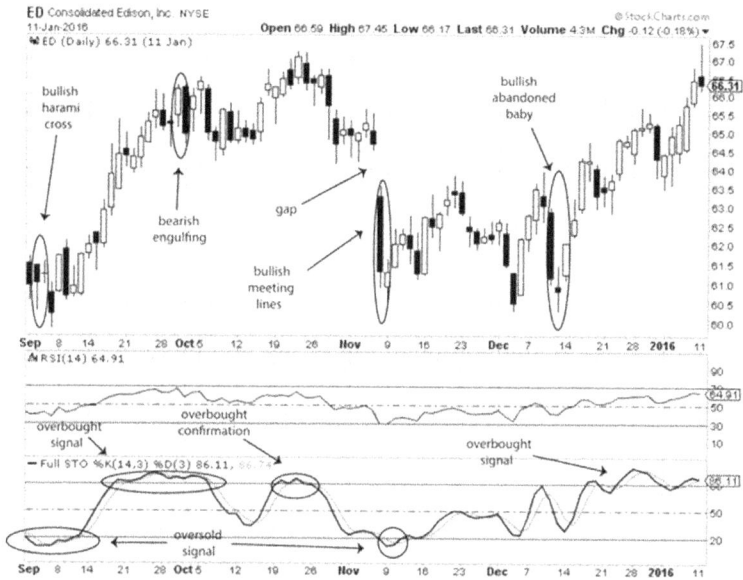

Figure 7.1 Stochastic as confirmation

In this chart, the price-based reversals are specific and easily identified. However, throughout the chart, RIS is of no immediate confirmation value. The index does not move outside of 70 to 30 range at any point. However, stochastic provides very strong signals. The initial price signal in the form of a bullish harami cross occurs in conjunction with stochastic moving averages both below 20, a clear bullish confirmation. As price rises, stochastic moves very strongly into overbought range and remains there for more than 2 weeks. At the same time, price reaches a plateau with the appearance of a bearish engulfing, a strong reversal signal. In this formation, the candlestick confirms what stochastic forecasts. Even so, price rises as stochastic retreats to midrange, finally moving once again into overbought right before price begins a sharp decline.

A fast reversal next occurs, starting with a large downside gap and exceptionally broad bullish meeting lines. Confirming these bullish signals is a brief movement of stochastic into oversold territory. As it often occurs, price does not react immediately but continues a sideways movement between $60 and $63. In mid-December, the bullish abandoned baby signals a new upward movement, which occurs immediately after. This sort of delayed reaction for price movement is not uncommon. Combining price signals with stochastic provides a degree of certainty in confirmation, however. Toward the end of the chart, as price continues rising, stochastic once again moves into the overbought range.

The value of reviewing stochastic along with RSI is in the confirmation this provides, notably in periods of volatility. This chart, although highly volatile, yielded many signals of superior strength, and confirmation occurred not in RSI, but in the stochastic oscillator.

Stochastic Identifying Reversal Points

As a measure of confirmation, stochastic may often be more insightful than RSI. As the previous example reveals, stochastic may even lead the signal to be confirmed by price (or volume or moving averages). Another value to stochastic is its use to pinpoint actual reversal points.

One of the truths not often discussed in technical literature is the problem of timing. Pointing to specific indicators as reversal signals is presumed to also reveal when to enter a trade. This is more elusive than many authors or academics would have you believe, however. In practice, timing is difficult. As the previous chart revealed, the signal might appear a month or longer before an actual reversal takes place. This is another problem that can be eased to a degree by observations of stochastic signals.

For example, in the chart in Figure 7.2, numerous moves in stochastic into overbought and oversold identify the likely points where trades should be entered—based on initial reversal signals and then on confirmation.

The first sign that this stock was overbought was seen in an extended move of stochastic into overbought range. This was confirmed by two brief moves in RSI, also into overbought territory. A lot of overbought indication foreshadows a bearish reversal, but at the same time, support was re-established at $78 per share. A true bearish signal would not occur if this held. The mid-November stochastic move all the way down to oversold predicted a brief move up about four points; but this was a minor retracement only and not a major move.

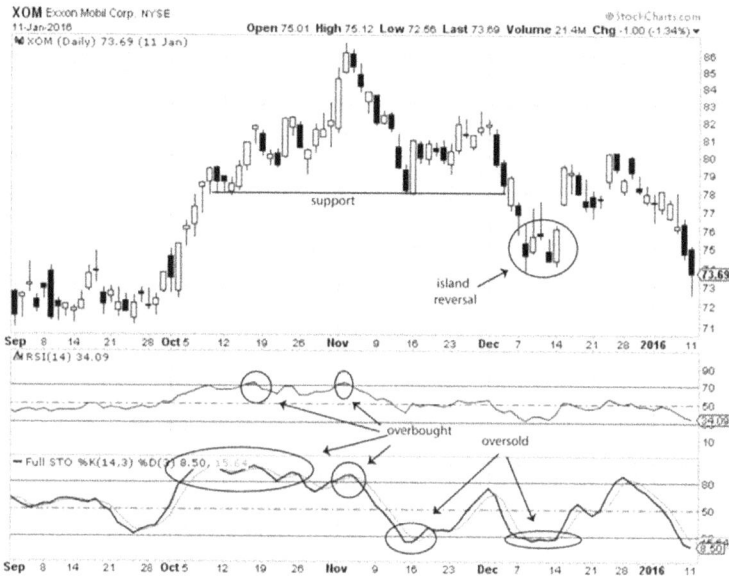

Figure 7.2 Stochastic identifying reversal points

A second oversold signal occurred in stochastic in December. How-ever, at the same time, price formed an island reversal, an unusual forma-tion characterized by a range of trading with gaps on either side, in this case below support. It can be interpreted as a bullish reversal like a double bottom or inverse head and shoulders. The bearish move in stochastic diverged from the bullish signal in price. The resulting move in price back above support looked at first like the island reversal was a true bullish signal and that stochastic was inaccurate, a false signal. However, by the conclusion of the chart, price again began trending lower and stochastic followed by again moving strongly all the way from overbought down to oversold.

In this difficult chart pattern, how can you anticipate a false or failing signal? Even with reversal and confirmation, anticipating price direction is never an exact science. One observation worth noting on this chart is the relatively brief movement into overbought and oversold, for both RSI and stochastic oscillators. Except for the first overbought move in stochas-tic, all these extremes were weak. Therefore, the indicators in price were especially difficult to read. This brings up a rule for chart interpretation: Just as strong reversal and confirmation signals are most likely to lead to reversal, by the same argument weak reversals and confirmation signals are *less* likely to succeed. It is also a key to accurate reading to pay attention to the proximity of reversal signals to resistance and support.

In the chart, most of the momentum and price signals occurred at or near the price range extremes. However, the signals themselves were weak, and the confirmation signals were also weak or worked more as divergence than confirmation. The logical conclusion is that the stochastic oscillator may be more valuable than RSI in identifying overbought and oversold conditions; but because it yields more signals, it is more susceptible to false readings as well. In the chart identifying reversal points, few of the momentum signals were compelling; and the only strong price signal was the island reversal, which also failed to reverse and hold.

The stochastic oscillator adds an element of value in confirming strong initial reversal signals seen elsewhere (e.g., in price signals like candlesticks and gaps). The oscillator is also useful in identifying reversal points. However, a weak reversal that is confirmed by equally weak signals is not reliable enough to enter a trade. The wise investor or trader will know to patiently wait for stronger signals to emerge.

The next chapter presents one final indicator with strong attributes for identifying reversal. The Bollinger Bands is a valuable addition to the family of oscillators and provides reversals even during periods of consolidation.

Class Questions for Discussion and/or Mini-Case Studies

Multiple Choice

1. The stochastic oscillator is
   (a) like RSI because it is based on 14 periods and identifies overbought and oversold conditions
   (b) dissimilar to RSI in the sense that it is based on three moving averages versus one
   (c) identifies 80 as overbought and 20 as oversold, versus RSI's 70/30 index
   (d) all of the above

2. The value of the stochastic is that
   (a) with two moving averages, signals occur more often than RSI's signals
   (b) it is virtually the same as RSI, and either can be employed with the same results
   (c) it always behaves as a leading indicator
   (d) it is easy to understand and makes moving average convergence divergence and RSI obsolete
3. The stochastic signal is of special interest when
   (a) the %K and %D are the same
   (b) the %K and %D signals move apart and create divergence
   (c) a single moving average is adequate to produce strong reversal signals
   (d) there are no other forms of confirmation available

Mini-Case Study

A chart has a series of short-term trends and reversals; however, RSI remains between 70 and 30 for the entire period. By adding stochastic to the chart, identify movement outside of the 80 to 20 range and note how these reversal signals result in actionable reversal signals.

CHAPTER 8

Bollinger Bands

Overview: Bollinger Bands is a momentum oscillator that tracks a simple moving average of price and presents a range of likely trading within two standard deviations, one above and one below. The power of Bollinger Bands is in its revelation of price deviation and likelihood of retracement once the bandwidth is violated. This makes Bollinger Bands the single most essential probability and momentum tracking signal available.

Bollinger Bands has been described as a volatility tracking signal, or even as a measure of probability. However, it serves as a hybrid that tests momentum in a very specific manner. It identifies the level of high or low prices in comparison to the previous or typical price range. This makes the Bollinger Bands a symptom of momentum because as the degree of change accelerates, the result is seen immediately in Bollinger signals.

The indicator consists of three moving averages, or bands. Developed by John Bollinger in the 1980s, this sets up a price overlay that reveals dynamic price trends and levels of resistance and support. The first band is the middle band, a simply moving average of price, calculated over the most recent 20 sessions. Second and third are the upper and lower bands, calculated as two standard deviations from the middle band. As volatility levels in price expand, the upper and lower bands widen, creating a visual representation of price volatility and of momentum in the price trend. The same applies when volatility declines. The upper and lower bands become narrower as volatility falls.

Bollinger Bands as a Visual Probability Signal

In most statistical exercises, a population is finite. The analysis consists of studying a fixed number of values in a field (voters, shoppers, or rolls of the dice). However, in stock prices, there are no fixed number of outcomes or, as statisticians would explain it, stock prices do not contain normal distribution. The number of possible variables is practically unlimited, based on fractional share prices at every point during a trading day, hour, or minute.

As a result, the well-known bell curve with its even distribution cannot be applied to probability in stock prices. The outcome of distribution will report many "fat tails," the tendency for variance to reflect extreme deviations and exceptions. The orderly bell curve based on a finite population is symmetrical, with a range of outcomes well understood. To analyze probability in stock prices, a different method must be applied. This is where Bollinger Bands becomes a valuable indicator of volatility and momentum. As a visual probability indicator, Bollinger Bands is designed to keep the usual price movement within the range of bands, which becomes a reflection of the likely price range over time. When the price begins to evolve, meaning moving to a higher or lower side of its range or trending outside of upper or lower bands, it indicates that momentum is increasing in the direction of movement. Price may also shrink as the trading range narrows, and this is reflected in a smaller range between upper and lower bands.

Calculating bands using standard deviation creates an exceptionally strong probability range; when price moves beyond these limits or when it behaves in an extreme manner of movement, the indication of coming price direction is strengthened. For example, in the chart in Figure 8.1,

Figure 8.1 Bollinger Bands directional signals

Bollinger Bands shows that during most of the chart, price evolves predictably within the confines of the upper and lower bands. However, on two occasions, price moves above the upper band. This is a sign of increasing bullish momentum. After the first move, price trended higher. The second instance confirmed the continuation of the bullish trend and the momentum behind that trend.

In both cases, the move above the upper band was preceded by an upward price gap. This could be interpreted as the cause for the move outside of the band range, making it a false signal. Price retraced immediately below the upper band. Through most of the chart, the price remained between the middle and upper bands, confirming the bullish momentum in this trend.

The single instance of price moving below the lower band has a similar characteristic, a series of downward gaps prior to the move below the lower band. This must be understood as part of a marketwide price decline which retraced quickly. Confirming this was the almost immediate move of price range back to the level between the middle and upper bands for most of the remaining period.

Another interpretation of the gaps in price and moves above the upper band can be to see this as a signal of a coming bullish trend. This occurred in the second instance, but not in the first. This demonstrates that when a new trend is expected, any signal (even as strong as a gap and move above upper band) needs strong confirmation in order to act on what appears to be taking place. In the second gap, the two sessions immediately following formed a bullish harami (black session and smaller white session); this could be considered bullish confirmation. However, in the first move above the upper band, the pattern along was followed by a bullish candlestick signal, the piercing lines (long black session followed by a smaller white session opening lower and advancing). However, even this confirmation was a false signal, as price did not advance. The moves outside of the outer bands are not reliable as trending signals, as these inconsistencies reveal.

Even so, the probability of price trends is richly indicated in many ways by Bollinger Bands. Numerous forms of signals aid traders in timing trades in anticipation of reversal that is likely to follow.

Calculation of the Three Bands

The three sections of the Bollinger Bands indicator are calculated using statistical methods. Based on the most often used 20-period calculation, the middle band is a simple moving average of closing prices for the past 20 sessions:

$$(P_1 + P_2 + \ldots P_{20}) \div 20 = MA$$

where P is the period
and MA the moving average (middle band).

The upper and lower bands are calculated using standard deviation. This involves six steps:

1. Calculate a moving average (see earlier), in this case for 20 periods.
2. Find the deviation for each session. This is the net difference between each session's closing price and the period's average price.
3. Square each session's deviation.
4. Add together all the squared values for the 20 periods.
5. Divide the total of squared values by the 20 periods to find the average.
6. Calculate the square root to arrive at the standard deviation.

To arrive at the complete Bollinger Bands indicator, the upper and lower bands are two standard deviations removed from the center band. Standard deviation is also referred to as Sigma, the Greek letter; and standard deviation is expressed as the square of Sigma, Σ^2: $(X - \mu)^2$.

Although the calculation of two standard deviations is complex, online charting services automatically make the calculations and reflect them on stock charts. It is important for traders to know how the calculation is performed, but it is not necessary to go through the tedious process of these six steps.

Bollinger Band Signals During Consolidation Trends

The application of Bollinger Bands is rarely discussed in technical analysis literature. The indicator normally is expressed solely in terms of how it interacts with price and what movement beyond upper and lower bands signifies. However, Bollinger Bands is more than just an anomaly related to price. It tracks momentum and expresses the probability of price behavior. Bollinger Bands, for this reason, is exceptionally valuable in identifying price activity, especially in one specific circumstance: the consolidation trend.

Consolidation, that time when prices are moving sideways rather than upward or downward, is seen by many as a problem. To some traders, when the trading breadth narrows and settles into a sideways movement, it is viewed as a period between dynamic trends, a pause of uncertainty during which no action can be taken. For those holding equity position, consolidation is a "wait and see" time or a time to sell long positions and seek a more dynamic position. However, this period of sideways movement is a trend. If viewed in this manner, the next task is to identify how (or if) a breakout can be identified. In fact, for many stocks, more time is taken up in consolidation than in bullish or bearish movement.

Interpreting consolidation is a challenging proposal. However, numerous signals can be applied to identify breakouts and anticipate price movement above or below consolidation. This requires a redefinition of "reversal." These may consist of a widening or narrowing range in consolidation, or failed breakouts as possible changes to the trend.

To most analysts, a reversal is believed possible only when a current trend is dynamic, either bullish or bearish. A reversal signal marks a spot where the trend is expected to stop and a new trend to begin moving in the opposite direction. This limits a trader's perspective because it recognizes only bullish and bearish price movement. However, if "reversal" is redefined to mean a change in the current trend to a different one, reversal signals can be used to mark the end of consolidation. In this respect, a reversal means the conclusion of the range-bound sideways movement, into a dynamic new movement, either bullish or bearish. It can also mean exchange of one consolidation plateau for another, either higher or lower.

For example, Figure 8.2 reveals a typical breakout from a 6-month consolidation. The trading range was restricted to a range between $59.50 and $64 per share. Then a series of strong downward runaway gaps broke through support, *reversing* consolidation for the first time in 6 months. The August 24 session with a large lower shadow is ignored

Figure 8.2 Breakout to new plateau

because this was the day of a marketwide decline. However, the change marked the beginning of a lower consolidation plateau between $56 and $59 per share.

This revised consolidation plateau lasted over 1 month, but a strong reversal signal appeared in the beginning of October in the form of a bullish engulfing signal. From this, you would expect price range to grow above the newly set resistance level of $59 per share. As the price moved out of the higher consolidation and settled into the lower one, Bollinger Bands expanded to a wide range, and then settled in, reverting again to the narrow range seen in the first consolidation trend. This reflected the unsettled volatility during the change.

In all of this, Bollinger Bands was a confirming force and the trading range was maintained between the upper and lower bands even with substantial price movement. Except for August 24 and 25, price remained within this well-defined range for the entire chart. Momentum was low during the first period of consolidation, expanding two points or less from upper to lower band. As the runaway gaps began, Bollinger range expanded substantially. This reflected greater volatility in price, but also of momentum in the runaway gap trend. Price in the third downward gapping session also moved below the lower band. Once the new consolidation period was set, the bandwidth also settled down. However, the appearance of the bullish engulfing pattern could be interpreted as a bullish reversal. How was this confirmed?

The answer is found in the expansion of this chart, as shown in Figure 8.3. Immediately following the candlestick bullish signal, price

Figure 8.3 Breakout to bullish trend

moved above the upper band and continued moving above for four sessions. Also note that trading remained between the upper band and the middle band over a period of 2 months. This clearly was a successful breakout from consolidation, to a new bullish trend.

The bullish trend lasted only 2 months and moved 10 points. At its beginning, price moved above the upper band, although only briefly. The trend ended and was marked by a reversal in the form of a bearish three inside down signal. The last session in this three-part signal also moved trading from the upper half (between middle and upper bands) on the Bollinger Bands to the lower (between middle and lower bands). Over the next few sessions, price moved below the lower band as a new bearish trend was set. Throughout the remainder of the period charted, price remained below the middle band.

These examples reveal the momentum attributes of Bollinger Bands and how they confirm price tendencies, both during a trend and at the point of reversal. They also demonstrated the tendency for the bands to define a trading range even when price behavior is volatile.

The Bollinger Squeeze

Another signal found in Bollinger Bands is called the *squeeze*. This is a tendency for price to narrow in the extreme on one side or the other of the bandwidth. It anticipates reversal out of consolidation and into a new dynamic trend. The expectation is that prices will move in the direction of the squeeze; as price narrows, it predicts continuation. The squeeze is

Figure 8.4 Bollinger squeeze

effective at pointing to likely breakout and continuation of a new trend, notably a breakout from consolidation.

For example, in Figure 8.4, consolidation's end is marked initially by a reversal in the form of a bullish inverted hammer. This is a 2-day candlestick consisting of a black session, a downside gap, and a white session with an upper shadow extended at least as far as the range of trading during that day. The bullish inverted hammer highlighted on the chart foreshadows upside movement. It is a powerful sign of reversal as the hammer's second day opens below support and immediately rises. However, how do you know whether this reversal will lead to a breakout?

Confirmation appears in the form of a Bollinger squeeze, a narrowing of the daily breadth of trading. Looking back to the period of consolidation, trading covered approximately three points; and the squeeze consisted of only fractional point ranges. Furthermore, the squeeze occurred in the upper segment of the bandwidth and moved above the upper band.

The pattern here demanded caution. Two attempts at breakout below support failed, so even the initial move above resistance had to be responded to with great care. A failed breakout was one possibility. However, as the squeeze continued into late November, the new bullish trend became firmly established (but not long-lasting). Price remained in the upper half of the bandwidth until the reversal at mid-December. Another reason for caution is that the squeeze is not 100 percent reliable, even as confirmation. Two additional squeezes can be observed, one each in late November and late December. Neither of these succeeded in setting up continued bullish moves. In fact, after the squeeze of late December, moving upward toward the middle band, price plummeted from $28 to $20 in only 2 weeks.

The Bollinger squeeze is noteworthy due to price tendency. As price breadth narrows, the tendency is for a breakout from consolidation and a widening reaction pattern. The narrowing range of the squeeze anticipates both breakout and expanded momentum. Closely associated with the Bollinger squeeze is the analysis of bandwidth. As this widens, it is associated with growing momentum. In the previous chart, this was seen during the month of November. In December, bandwidth began narrowing, anticipating the strong bearish reversal that followed. The combined analysis of Bollinger squeeze and bandwidth augments momentum analysis and aids in your ability to anticipate reversal.

However, that same narrowing of bandwidth can be deceptive. If bandwidth narrows in a manner anticipating reversal and confirmation is also found, it is a reliable signal. But in this case, narrowing was confusing because it also formed new squeezes, both ending in failure. The signal is by no means a certain one of momentum or of price reversal to follow.

M Tops and W Bottoms

Within Bollinger Bands, another set of signals is like the well-known double top and double bottom. Variations of these well-known signals are the M top and W bottom. These contain the same reversal significance as double tops and bottoms, but with a different price pattern in between the peaks. Double tops and bottoms tend to occur near one another; price in the M and W patterns retreated and turns, forming the letter shapes. In technical analysis, the failure to continue movement in one direction usually translates to reaction moves in the opposite direction. This is true of double tops and bottoms and equally of M tops and W bottoms. Momentum in one direction reverses once price movement fails.

Figure 8.5 provides an example of these patterns. The W bottom appears first with price falling below lower band at the second leg. The move above the upper band at the middle portion augments the volatility in this price pattern, but the W bottom is as strong, if not stronger than the more common double bottom pattern.

Figure 8.5 **M top and W bottom**

Price levels peaked as the M top appeared. Like the double top, the M top is a bearish reversal formation. The price reaction was strong, moving below the lower band over several sessions. The M top and W bottom aid in management of exceptionally volatile patterns. In this example, Bollinger Bands expanded at the start of the W bottom and again at the end of the M top. Although this bandwidth activity is not as predictable as other Bollinger signals, it is one symptom of growing momentum during a volatile period.

A danger in locating W bottoms and M tops is that the appearance may easily represent a coincidence of price behavior, without a true predictive value. Like many Western technical signals, notably triangles and wedges, the value of what a trader sees often is affected by expectation. The W and M patterns should be strongly confirmed by other signals. Is it truly a signal of shifts in momentum and price reversal to follow? Without confirmation, this cannot be known.

Bollinger Bands Tracking Resistance and Support

Another use of Bollinger Bands is the tracking of either resistance or support. Although this application is related more to price trend than to momentum, the slope of the trading borders is an indication of the momentum level in effect at the time. The stronger and more rapid the price movement, the stronger the signal of increasing momentum; and if the slope of resistance or support slows down, it is a further indicator of slowing momentum. In this sense, price may serve as an initial indicator, to be confirmed by other signals found in momentum oscillators.

Using Bollinger Bands in this way also helps identify flexible resistance and support ranges, which are not always going to move in a straight line. For example, the chart in Figure 8.6 shows how the upper Bollinger Band closely tracks resistance, even during periods of rising and falling trading levels.

The narrow bandwidth combined with narrow trading range is a symptom of low momentum through most of this period. Bollinger Bands provides two benefits here: tracking resistance even during small increase or decrease in trading levels; and confirmation of low volatility. The one spike in volatility from August to September was the result of the August 24 marketwide 1-day crash. Resistance is tracked closely by the upper band as price rises. The greater the momentum of price increase and resulting slope of price, the more closely the upper band tracks. This was true especially during the month of October.

Bollinger Bands also tracks support. Figure 8.7 reveals a considerably different level of momentum even as the lower band closely follows the price support level.

In this case, price is declining sharply throughout the period, from $135 down to $83. Although the lower band closely tracks support, the changes in bandwidth were a symptom of growing momentum in this bearish price trend. As with resistance on the price rise, when the price decline was strong, the lower band tracked support closely. The first half of December demonstrated this tendency.

Figure 8.6 Bollinger Bands tracking resistance

Figure 8.7 Bollinger Bands tracking support

Without the use of the lower band to track support, this level could be difficult to identify when relying on price alone. The repetitive price jumps and retracements (another sign of high momentum) made it difficult to identify support. At the same time, price breadth was low for most of this period, interrupted by occasional higher breadth and price gaps. In this period of uncertainty, Bollinger Bands identified support as well as momentum in the bearish trend. At the same time, price resided in the lower half of the bandwidth, between the middle band and the lower band. The occasional moves above the middle band led to retracement to the downside every time, without exception. These moves above, combined with retracement below, are marked on the chart.

Yet another useful application of Bollinger Bands is found when the default of two standard deviations is replaced by three. Movement above a three-deviation upper band or below a three-deviation lower band is rare; but when it occurs, retracement back into range will be immediately in almost every case. This means that once the bands are violated, timing a trade in anticipation of retracement will almost always be well timed.

Three Standard Deviations

The default of two standard deviations is widely accepted as a reliable form of Bollinger Bands. The preceding charts revealed that moves above the upper band or below the lower band are rare and short-lived. This alone makes Bollinger Bands a formidable tracking indicator of both price and momentum.

Figure 8.8 Bollinger Bands with 3 standard deviation setting

If the default of two standard deviations is replaced with three, violations of the bandwidth will not be found in most charts. However, if it is found, the likelihood of immediate retracement is nearly 100 percent certain. No signal can provide 100 percent confidence, but the three standard deviation application of Bollinger Bands is as close as possible.

For example, in Figure 8.8, price was volatile, but only two instances of violation of the lower band occurred, lasting only 1 to 2 days each. This is typical movement outside of the bandwidth for three standard deviations is rare and sets up strong likelihood of immediate retracement.

The t-line

Bollinger Bands can be used to set up unusually strong price channels as well. In this application, the t-line is added to Bollinger Bands to set up the signal. As soon as price moves outside of the established channel, it signals a change in price and a corresponding change in momentum.

The t-line is an 8-day exponential moving average of price. The observation most often applied to the t-line when observed by itself involved price crossover. When the t-line moves above price and closes above for at least 2 days, it signals a bullish reversal; when the t-line moves below price and closes below for at least 2 days, it signals a bearish reversal. Most often used alone, the t-line is often promoted as an exceptionally reliable signal. However, numerous false signals are produced by the t-line. It is based on an exceptionally short-term moving average, making it unreliable and not strong enough to set up a trade. An observation of the t-line establishes this.

The chart in Figure 8.9 shows how the t-line is superimposed over price. It tracks price closely, as you would expect when using only an 8-day moving average. However, identifying the difference between reversal and retracement is difficult.

For example, five instances of crossover, all lasting 2 days or more, are highlighted on the chart. All were false signals. A trader acting on these crossover signals would have made an ill-timed decision.

When t-line is combined with Bollinger Bands, a powerful and reliable combined trend develops in the form of narrow channels. An example of this is shown by taking the same chart and adding Bollinger Bands, as shown in Figure 8.10.

Figure 8.9 t-line

Figure 8.10 t-line with Bollinger Bands

Two specific channels are highlighted in this chart. The bearish move combines the t-line as resistance and the lower band as support. The bullish move combines the t-line as support and the upper band as resistance. In both cases, the channels are reliable in tracking momentum for as long as the price range remains within the channels. However, as soon as the price moves outside of the channel, the reversal is signaled immediately. This occurred on December 26 and 27 when price turned and crossed above the channel range; and again on March 7 and 8, marking the end of the bullish trend. In both instances, the crossover closed across the line for 2 days, which was the signal that the current trend had ended.

The combination of t-line and Bollinger Bands accurately marks the combined change in momentum and price and can be used to identify the point where reversal begins. Confirmation may be found in additional price or momentum signals as this occurs.

The next section introduces the last set of chapters, addressing the use of momentum oscillators to aid in trading, including timing of trades based on momentum signals and confirmation.

Class Questions for Discussion and/or Mini-Case Studies

Multiple Choice

1. Bollinger Bands consists of
   (a) an exponential moving average of price
   (b) a simple moving average of price for a lengthy period
   (c) a simple moving average and upper and lower bands based on two standard deviations from the middle band
   (d) none of the above

2. Movements of price above the upper band or below the lower band
   (a) are likely to be followed by retracement back into range
   (b) always reflect growing momentum and a continuing trend in the same direction
   (c) can be ignored because they occur often
   (d) never occur due to the statistical strength of standard deviation analysis

3. The Bollinger squeeze refers to
   (a) a tendency for price to remain in low volatility due to the nature of standard deviation
   (b) market pressures on the indicator, making it less reliable
   (c) a tendency for price range to narrow as a price trend begins
   (d) pressures from buyers and sellers, resulting in extremely low price range

True or False

1. The M top and W bottom are like double tops and bottoms.
2. When the default is changed to three standard deviations, it makes Bollinger Bands ineffective.
3. Bollinger Bands tracks resistance and support, often more effectively than a single line used in traditional analysis.

Discussion

Find a stock chart and identify the following: movement of price above the upper band, movement below the lower band, an M top and W bottom, the Bollinger squeeze, and tracking of resistance and support. Explain and identify each of these events and demonstrate the results in terms of price behavior that followed.

PART III

Trading with Momentum Oscillators

CHAPTER 9

Coordinating Oscillators with Other Indicators

Overview: Oscillators are effectively used along with volume and price indicators. The oscillator judges the strength and speed of price activity, but not the direction. Thus, it may be an initial signal or a confirmation of other signals. Traders must recognize the value as well as the limitations of momentum and need to rely on a set of different signal types for signal and confirmation.

No oscillator or any other indicator should ever be relied upon by itself. Confirmation is required before any trade is entered, because nothing works 100 percent of the time. Even the most reliable signal may be a false signal, representing a coincidence of behavior in price, volume, moving averages, and momentum.

What are the most reliable forms of confirmation? An oscillator can be confirmed by another oscillator as a starting point. For example, stochastic and relative strength index (RSI) work well together as signal and cross-confirmation. However, because of their similarities, this is not a universally reliable form of confirmation. Momentum is not related directly to price direction, but rather serves as a measure of the speed and strength of the trend. You need more than only a momentum-based reversal signal.

The combined use of Bollinger Bands and the t-line is one example of expanding signal reliability. As a momentum oscillator, Bollinger Bands provides strong and usually reliable signaling benefits; but it is not always adequate by itself. The t-line is a short-term and weak price signal when analyzed without added information. Combining Bollinger Bands and the t-line sets up a powerful channel track and momentum tracing signal.

Beyond the use of such signals, traders may confirm momentum using other volume and price signals.

Volume Spikes and Indicators

The Dow theory states as one of its tenets that volume leads price. This is often true, but an observation of repetitive price patterns shows that it is more likely that price and volume signals often occur at the same time and work well together to signal changes in momentum. Most easily spotted among volume signals is the simple one-session or two-session volume spike.

Many analysts have noted that the price reversal and volume spike, when taking place together, are among the strongest of reversal signals. This is not the end of the discussion, however. A truly powerful reversal signal is found when three reversals occur together: price indicator, volume spike, and momentum overbought or oversold.

In the chart in Figure 9.1, several strong reversal signals forecast a downtrend. Three price-related signals occurred in a short span of five sessions. These were the piercing lines, a large price gap, and a harami. The unusual price activity also formed an island cluster, confirming the likelihood of a bearish reversal.

Figure 9.1 Three-part reversal signals

Additional confirmation was seen in the exceptionally sharp volume spike. In the entire period shown, this was the single largest volume session, and such extremes often accompany reversal. The final confirmation was found in RSI, which moved above 70 and into the overbought range of the index. This was the only incidence in the chart when the momentum reported overbought.

These signals all combined to forecast a coming downtrend. After a pause for the rest of November, the downtrend began and continued into late January.

Numerous volume signals further augment the ability to confirm momentum and price signals. Mastering these adds further power to forecasting and identification of reversal in price trends.

Western and Eastern Price Signals

A price signal is normally thought of as an initial reversal, to be confirmed by other price signals, momentum, volume, or moving averages. However, in some cases, momentum will act as a leading indicator and price will then confirm the predicted reversal. The same is true for volume, which may lead price. One of the more valuable reversal signals is a combination of volume and momentum, which then may be confirmed and followed by price.

A case in which this occurs is shown in Figure 9.2. In this chart, the stochastic oscillator led each example of reversal. The first two were oversold, and the third was an extended period in which the stock was overbought.

The first two oscillator moves into oversold were initially confirmed by volume spikes. However, it was only after these developments that price gave out a confirming indicator. The bullish engulfing was an exceptionally strong reversal signal, normally thought of as a leading indicator. In this example, it confirmed the momentum and volume forecasts and was a delayed reaction a month after the price reached a bottom. It also set up a flip from resistance to support, one of the strongest forms of confirmation.

The third stochastic signal was overbought for 1 full month, which is unusual. Price reacted next with two small hanging man signals, which

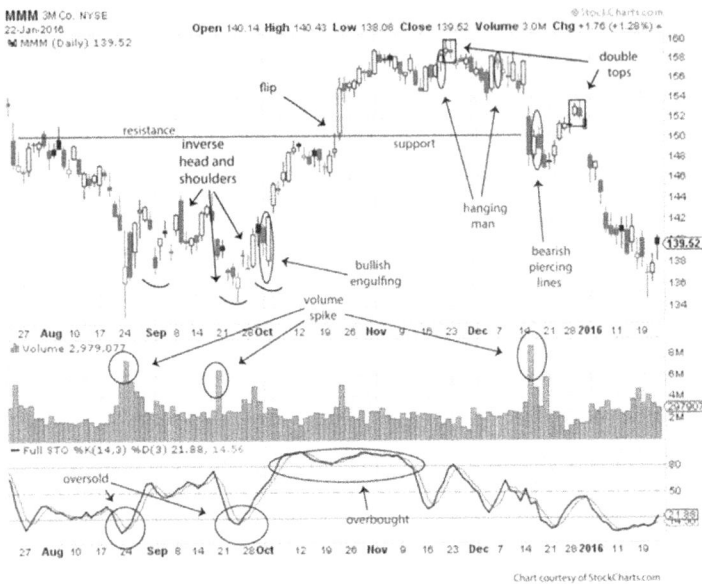

Figure 9.2 Momentum and volume as leading indicators

are bearish reversals appearing at or near the top of a bullish trend. How-ever, the result was not immediate. The final volume spike was convincing because it occurred as price moved below the newly established support level; and this was followed immediately by the bearish piercing lines, confirming the bearish reversal.

In each of these cases, price was the final leg in a series of reversal signals and confirmation provided by momentum and volume. It is a mistake to assume that price always leads a reversal and that momentum must occur in a nonprice signal of one kind or another. As this exercise reveals, the process of reversal and confirmation is flexible and may occur in any variety of sequences.

The same observations will apply just as well to noncandlestick price reversals. For example, the pattern in the chart from September 1 through the first two October sessions are identified as an inverse head and shoulders pattern, a bullish signal. In fact, this led to a strong bull-ish move that took price through the flip from resistance to support. Another example was found in November 20 and 23, in which a double top formed. Although these were small, they were in the perfect place, at the top of the range. Another double top formed at the top of the reaction high at December 29 and 30. This confirmed the downtrend and revealed that the 6-day upward move was only a retracement and not a true reversal.

This busy chart makes the case that there is no shortage of indicators if a trader is willing to look at every form of signal: price, volume, moving average, and momentum. A common error is to develop a short list of favorite signals, and to become blinded to less familiar ones. It is not an easy task, but complete analysis of a chart must include signals from all possible sources.

The next chapter takes this a step further, demonstrating the many ways that reversal and confirmation will be found on a chart.

Class Questions for Discussion and/or Mini-Case Studies

Multiple Choice

1. A volume spike is one of the strongest of reversals and consists of
    (a) trend development marked by increasing daily volume
    (b) volatility in the volume from one day to the next
    (c) low volume accompanied by high price volatility
    (d) a 1-day or 2-day increase in volume, followed by more typical volume levels
2. The Dow theory states that
    (a) volume is a secondary factor after price
    (b) volume often acts as a leading indicator and price follows
    (c) price sets the pace but is not reliable as a leading indicator
    (d) momentum is usually an initial signal of reversal
3. Price reversal is characterized by
    (a) price leading the change, followed by confirmation in volume
    (b) price acting as a confirming indicator in all cases
    (c) price acting either as an initial indicator or as confirmation
    (d) momentum as an initial signal, confirmed by volume or price

Discussion

Identify on a stock chart examples of (a) price as the initial indicator, confirmed by volume or momentum, and (b) momentum as the initial indicator, confirmed by price or volume. Also identify a point where all three signals—price, volume, and momentum—act in conjunction to mark the point of reversal.

CHAPTER 10

Reversal Signals and Confirmation

Overview: Reversal does not always refer to a change from bull to bear or vice versa. Those are price directions. Reversal may also mean a reversal of the existing trend to a different trend, to or from consolidation. This form of reversal is most easily identified and spotted through subtle but important changes in momentum.

Given the many ways in which reversal signals appear and combine, how much do you need to make a well-timed trade? The answer lies in confirmation. Many correlations in signals and how they can be employed are often based in momentum. Some observations concerning the nature of reversal:

1. *Strength in trends leads to strength is reversal signal.* The greater the momentum is in the initial trend, the more likely it is to find strong reversal signals.
2. *Weakness in trends leads to weakness in signals.* A weak trend will eventually reverse. However, the initial weakness translates to equally weak signals. Slow momentum is not isolated but extends to slow reversal signals as well.
3. *Levels of strength in reversal signals are associated with the same levels in confirmation.* A reversal signal is most likely to be confirmed by signals of similar strength or weakness. This is also a symptom of momentum within the price movement.
4. *The strength in reversal tends to be met with equal strength in new trends.* This is a momentum factor as well. You will observe that opposite-moving trends tend to move at similar speed and last for similar duration as the preceding trend.

These observations aid traders in identifying when or when not to make trades, either to enter positions or to exit. Trend analysis with momentum in mind is aided by acknowledging the tendency for momentum to consistently remain in effect with reversal. It would not be logical to assume that momentum concludes merely because price changes direction.

Confirmation with Oscillators

The correlation of many signals is a requirement for effective charting. The patterns of price change—duration, direction, strength, or weakness—tend to develop as a repetitive factor within the same chart. This is true for all types of signals. Momentum oscillators often define the correlation factor in their own patterns.

The chart in Figure 10.1 is an example of this repetitive pattern tendency. In this chart, not only are the price patterns similar in duration, the confirmation in oscillators is also repetitive.

This chart is worthy of detailed analysis because it demonstrates the confirmation value of momentum oscillators and because it shows how

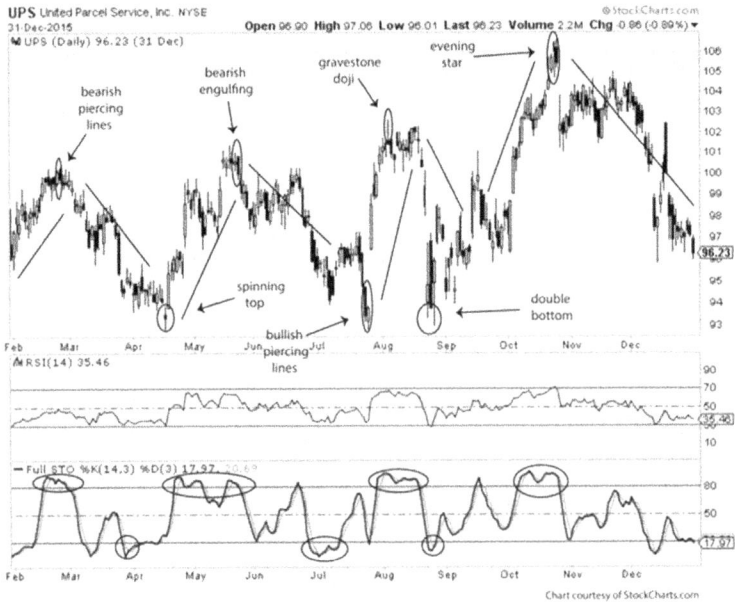

Figure 10.1 Oscillators confirming price correlation

price patterns are predictable in many charts, in terms of signals, high and low levels, and duration from start to finish.

The first noteworthy pattern is price itself. The durations of the short-term trends are remarkably similar, each about 1 month long. Second, each reversal is marked clearly with a signal of considerable strength. The bearish signals include piercing lines, engulfing, gravestone doji, and an evening star; all appear at the peak of the trend. The bullish signals include a spinning top, piercing lines, and a double bottom; all appear at the bottom of the trend.

All these price signals could be confirmed by other price signals upon more detailed examination. However, an equally powerful form of confirmation is found in momentum. The relative strength index (RSI) indicator is not especially revealing, as it never moves outside of the index range between 70 and 30. Even so, movement above or below the center-line tracks price closely enough to provide some indication of the levels of overbought or oversold that could evolve. But there is not enough strength in RSI to provide actionable buy or sell signals.

The stochastic oscillator, on the other hand, provides a powerful form of confirmation. In some of the reversals, momentum leads price and anticipates the direction's turn. This was the case in the first bearish reversal of late February; the second bullish reversal in July; and the third bearish reversal in August. In all these cases, the stochastic $\%K$ and $\%D$ both moved outside of midrange before price turned.

From this analysis, several conclusions can be drawn. First, price trends contained predictably similar levels of momentum. This is reflected both in the visual price chart and in the stochastic movements above and below midrange. Second, stochastic was of greater predictive value than RSI in this volatile pattern. Third, the consistency between price pattern and momentum was noteworthy, demonstrating that the use of momentum to confirm price may be a more reliable system than focusing solely on price-based confirmation.

Reversal from Consolidation Trends

For most traders, changes in dynamic trends—from bullish to bearish or vice versa—are easily spotted and acted upon. However, the reversal from range-bound consolidation to a different trend (either dynamic or a different consolidation plateau) is more challenging. Reversal is thought to be so difficult in these circumstances that many traders move to the sidelines during consolidation, waiting for a new dynamic trend to develop. This creates many lost opportunities. Momentum is the key to managing consolidation and spotting likely breakouts.

The chart in Figure 10.2 shows movement in one consolidation plateau to another, while support flips to resistance. The initial breakout is anticipated by a bearish rising wedge that forms into an island cluster.

Upon formation of the new, lower plateau, another island cluster forms and breaks out above resistance, only to retreat into range. By themselves, these price developments would be difficult to read. However, when momentum is added to the mix, the price movements are strongly confirmed by moving average convergence divergence (MACD) crossover. There were four instances of crossover marking the beginning and end of the second and third island clusters. This chart is an example of how momentum works with price trends and, in this instance, how breakouts fail.

The identification of breakout signals during consolidation is most difficult, more so than in dynamic trends. The specific price signals, accompanied by momentum, are efficient in spotting such changes.

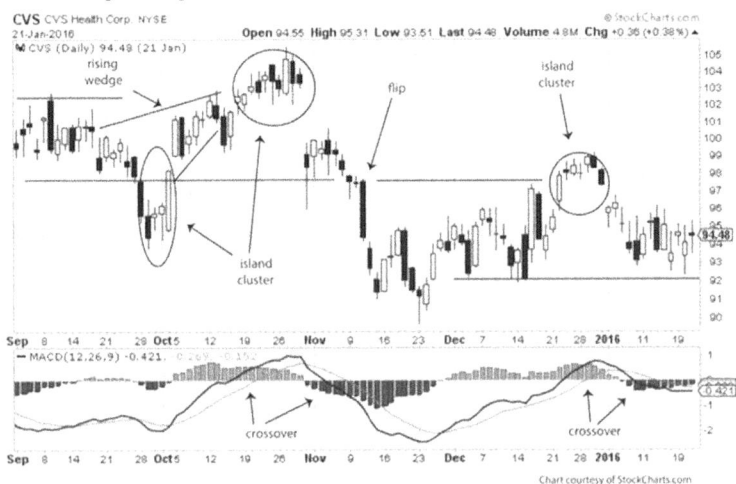

Figure 10.2 *Momentum signals during consolidation*

For example, the rising wedge and second island cluster forecast downward movement, but does this mean a downside breakout can endure? Once the momentum crossover appears and price broke out, the MACD moved down strongly, providing a clue that the newly established range was likely to hold.

Just as reversals require confirmation, so do continuation signals. A confusing aspect of literature on charting is the use of the word "continuation." It is often intermixed with consolidation as if the two terms were the same. However, whereas consolidation is a sideways trend, continuation is a signal indicating that the current trend will not end in the immediate future. This type of formation, found in both candlestick and traditional Western technical price signals, must be confirmed before it can be reliably used to have faith in the price trend. Momentum is a major consideration in determining whether the price trend will continue or, if it does, whether it is beginning to weaken. The next chapter addresses this question.

Class Questions for Discussion and/or Mini-Case Studies

Multiple Choice

1. A price reversal
   (a) refers to a change from bullish to bearish, or from bearish to bullish
   (b) refers to any change from an existing trend to a new trend.
   (c) is always dynamic in nature, never sideways
   (d) is enough by itself to enter a trade

2. Consolidation is
   (a) a trend moving sideways
   (b) a period of indecision, when traders must wait for a new trend to begin
   (c) a period in between bullish or bearish trends
   (d) when prices are range-bound but on the verge of breaking out

3. Continuation refers to
   (a) sideways-moving price ranges
   (b) the likely further move in the current trend

   (c) the second signal verifying the legitimate forecast of an initial signal

   (d) recurring signals leading to reversal

Discussion

Find examples on a stock chart of a consolidation trend and mark resistance and support. Also locate signals leading to likely breakout and the beginning of a new bullish, bearish, or consolidation trend.

CHAPTER 11

Continuation Signals and Confirmation

Overview: Continuation signals predict that current trends are most likely to continue. These appear during bullish or bearish trends and are considered reliable. However, more skill is required in interpreting continuation trends within a consolidation (sideways-moving) trend. Many traders believe that no forms of signals are reliable in this situation but adding momentum to the analysis makes it possible to spot continuation trends during consolidation.

Most technical analysts focus on reversal signals, but this excludes equally important continuation signals. This creates a problem for analysts and traders. Continuation, the tendency for a trend to continue in the same direction until a reversal occurs, is as important as reversal. However, traders may tend to ignore this, preferring to look only for reversal signals. Several assumptions add to this tendency, including the following:

1. *Confirmation bias.* The first and most important assumption is that a trend will always reverse when a strong signal is located. This leads to a failure to recognize continuation signals, and to not recognize the possibility of failed reversal signals. Confirmation bias is common in the market and may be one of the most difficult attributes to overcome. Traders, like most people, tend to hold onto their beliefs whether true or provably false. This may have a blinding effect on the ability to make rational trading decisions or to interpret technical information accurately.

2. *A belief in only the dynamic trend.* Many technical analysts recognize only two types of trends, bullish and bearish. Besides these dynamic trends, the sideways continuation is a form of nondynamic trend.

Thinking of this only as a pause between trends leads to missed opportunities for traders. Traders are impatient in general and are not prone to acceptance of subtle signals, such as consolidation trends. Most will prefer to wait for a new bullish or bearish trend before making decisions; many with current positions will prefer to close them even if it means taking a net loss, rather than to remain in a position without movement.

3. *Confusion about the definition of "continuation."* To many, continuation is not a trend but a period of uncertainty about the pricing of stock or even of agreement between buyers and sellers concerning the current range of trading. Both have a degree of truth, but the belief ignores the reality of continuation as a third type of trend. This is a view of the trading world requiring constant movement and activity, but one ignoring the reality: For many companies, more time is spent with price in a range-bound consolidation trend than in bullish or bearish movement. Ironically, this may be translated to mean that consolidation is "normal," and dynamic trends are the exceptions when volatility draws price levels into question.

4. *A belief that reversal signals in the wrong proximity represent continuation.* A reversal (especially of the candlestick variety) is valid only when it appears in the right proximity. This means a bullish signal must occur at the bottom of a downtrend and a bearish signal at the top of an uptrend. If these signals occur in the wrong place, they are not continuation signals, but only pattern coincidence. This misunderstanding reflects a desire for some form of signal among traders, and a frustration when signals do not point to action the trader wants to take. This tendency leads to ill-advised decisions or reliance on signals that are not signals at all, but merely a coincidence of patterns.

5. *A low level of understanding.* Chartists may suffer from a limited recognition of signals and fail to realize the power of continuation as a force within the trend. For example, most traders use candlestick charts to track their holdings; however, they may have a limited understanding of candlestick signals and what they mean. Traders may also have little or no understanding of relative degrees of strength or weakness in price signals; this carries over to an equally low appreciation for strength or weakness in momentum.

Continuation from Dynamic Trends

In a bullish or bearish trend, the unending challenge is to determine when a reversal will occur. Finding a strong continuation signal answers part of the question. Continuation not only confirms an initial reversal when the price moves above resistance or below support, it also forecasts that the trend is likely to continue for the moment. These moves outside the trading range are expected to reverse in most cases. However, finding and confirming continuation allows a trader to take exception to the idea that reversal will occur and to exploit the successful breakout.

Reversal from a dynamic trend is easily spotted. By the same argument, continuation is a powerful form of signal that confirms a breakout and new trading range. When continuation price signals are accompanied by momentum oscillator signals, they are much stronger. However, in reversal you expect to find overbought or oversold signals. For continuation, momentum confirms a signal when there is a lack of movement outside of the middle index. When the index value does not move into overbought or oversold, it confirms a continuation signal in price.

The chart in Figure 11.1 provides an example of price reversal and continuation signals, with confirmation in both relative strength index (RSI) and stochastic oscillators.

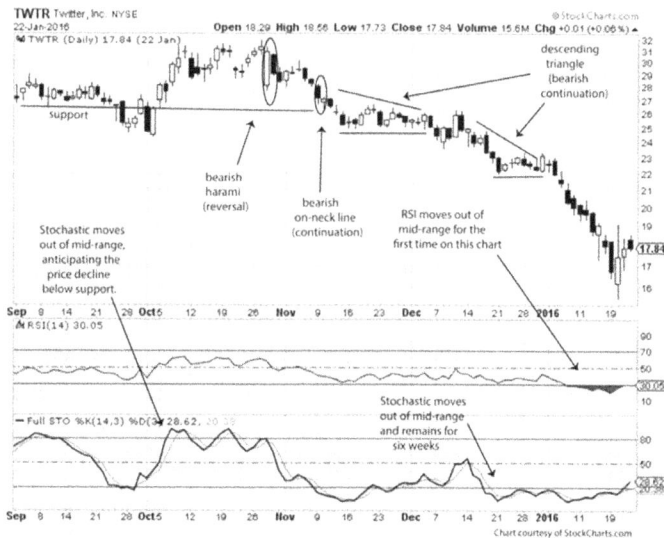

Figure 11.1 Momentum confirming continuation

The initial bearish harami reversal signal was not particularly strong, but it led to a drop in price below support. The on-neck continuation added confirmation that the bearish breakout and reversal was likely to hold. This was further confirmed by two descending triangles, which are strong bearish continuation indicators.

The activity in the two momentum indicators added further confirmation of the bearish continuation. First, RSI remained in midrange throughout the chart and did not move to oversold until early January. If RSI remained at midrange, it confirmed the legitimate bearish trend as likely to continue.

Stochastic was more volatile, as observed in previous chapters. However, the oscillator moves above and below midrange were brief on this chart, indicating that the price trend was not exaggerated in either direction. In late December, stochastic index moved into oversold territory and remained there for 6 weeks, indicating a likely end to the downtrend.

Continuation from Consolidation Trend Breakouts

Continuation signals such as those revealed in the chart apply equally during breakout from a consolidation trend. In previous chapters, the patterns were demonstrated for reversal, in which the range-bound price succeeds in breaking higher or lower. Confirmation in the form of momentum oscillators added confidence to the success of such breakouts.

By the same argument, when consolidation is the prevailing trend, a lack of movement into overbought or oversold reveals a likelihood that no breakout is on the horizon. This lack of change signal aids in determining when breakout is less likely. It confirms the likely continuation of the sideways-moving trend.

The same theory applies when breakouts from consolidation are confirmed. The major difference is that in order to confirm that a newly established price range makes sense, the oscillators should show no move out of midrange. They should remain in mid-index until the new trading range has been established as a successful one. In all cases of momentum used to confirm continuation, the confirmation comes in the form of a nonsignal. In other words, momentum does not become extreme, and when accompanied by price-specific continuation signals, momentum strengthens the likely continuation of a new trend.

All signals require confirmation in order to be viewed as legitimate. This applies to both reversal and continuation patterns. Momentum too is often overlooked at adding strength to reversals (by moves into overbought or oversold) or continuation (a lack of movement out of midrange). This is a mistake. Momentum oscillators may be viewed as providing an exceptional form of confirmation for all types of price movements.

The science of chart reading combines observation of many different signals and patterns. Most traders and analysts focus on price signals and reversal. However, numerous other signals (moving average, volume, and momentum) are equally important; and beyond reversal confirmation, trend continuation improves analysis of the chart. This is often discounted because a preference for reversal is the focus of nearly all chart analysis. When momentum is added to the effort, a much richer science evolves as a result.

It is disturbing that the focus on price reversal signals excludes consideration of other, equally powerful matters. Momentum oscillators are probably the most overlooked of all stock chart signals, probably because they are also the least understood. Momentum is not concerned with direction of price, but with speed and strength. This lack of focus on direction points to a cultural problem in all analysis. Stock watchers want to find signals anticipating direction and, specifically, reversal of direction. The market is a directionally biased place and most traders lose interest in any matter not related to the direction of price movement. Those analysts and traders who appreciate the value of momentum analysis are likely to benefit, simply from having in their possession a richer body of information.

Class Questions for Discussion and/or Mini-Case Studies

True or False

1. Momentum is only possible while a bullish or bearish trend is underway.
2. Consolidation is a third type of trend, beyond bullish or bearish.
3. In consolidation, the lack of signal in momentum is itself a signal.

Discussion

Find a chart with a consolidation trend and breakout. Compare and comment on the role of price signals as continuation of the success of a breakout and find confirmation within momentum oscillators.

Answers to Questions

Chapter 1

Multiple choice:

1. C
2. A
3. C

Discussion: Encourage the development of analytical skill and comfort with a variety of technical indicators. Students should be able to find price, volume, and momentum signals for initial and confirming signs. They should also be able to locate signs of weakening momentum in a trade, based solely on the slope of the trend as it nears exhaustion.

The skills required for exceptional charting analysis are the result of efforts beyond this introductory chapter. This discussion is a starting point for identifying student comfort with stock charts and a wide variety of signals.

Chapter 2

Multiple choice:

1. A
2. C
3. B
4. B

Discussion: Look for clear thinking and analytical ability. RWH, if accurate, should be reflected in a random pattern in price and the lack of long-term trends. Arguments in favor of RWH would have to be based on a truly random appearance in the chart. Arguments against would point to clear long-term trends, which statistically contradict the RWH idea.

Chapter 3

Multiple choice:

1. D
2. B
3. C

Discussion: In times of growing volatility, a trader faces increasing uncertainty. In this condition, MA analysis may point to reversal forecasting, and this is confirmed with the overlay of Bollinger Bands. Look for student answers demonstrating analytical skills that combine these indicators, and point to both crossover and movement outside of the Bollinger bandwidth. The purpose of this exercise is to enable students to articulate what constitutes valid signals and trend turning points.

Chapter 4

Multiple choice:

1. C
2. A
3. C
4. B

Discussion: Observe whether students have grasped the concept of RSI and the necessity of confirmation in the form of price or volume signals. The charts students select should clearly demonstrate the workings of RSI and how it is used to time entry and exit trades.

Chapter 5

Multiple choice:

1. D
2. B
3. B

Mini case study: Aid students in developing analytical skills and chart interpretation. In this exercise, a subtle distinction is made between the usual form of signal and confirmation (price confirmed by moves in RSI) and divergence with MACD contradicting what at first appears to be underway.

Chapter 6

Multiple choice:

1. C
2. A
3. D

True or false:

1. T
2. F
3. F

Discussion: Students should be able to find a chart with three specific attributes. These are a short-term price trend that is either confirmed by RSI or lacking a useful RSI signal, and a divergence signal from ROC. The student should be able to demonstrate that the ROC divergence predicted a reversal that otherwise was not visible.

Chapter 7

Multiple choice:

1. D
2. A
3. B

Mini-case study: Students should be able to identify distinct differences in signals between RSI and stochastic. By identifying strong reversals and confirmation based on price and stochastic, the student should appreciate the added value in this oscillator. At the same time, students should also be able to observe weak signals and confirmation and note the higher incidence of signal failure in those cases.

Chapter 8

Multiple choice:

1. C
2. A
3. C

True or false:

1. T
2. F
3. T

Discussion: These attributes of Bollinger Bands are critically essential to complete momentum analysis. Expect students to observe the patterns of price movement, price squeeze, and tracking of resistance and support. Also expect students to correctly interpret these price patterns and to describe how the resulting price reactions were predicted in the observed price behavior.

Chapter 9

Multiple choice:

1. D
2. B
3. C

Discussion: Students should demonstrate the ability to find the indicated signaling combinations on a chart. Because this skill is an advanced one, students excel when they are able to display insights into how price, volume, and momentum work together to strongly confirm reversal.

Chapter 10

Multiple choice:

1. B
2. A
3. B

Discussion: Students should be able to identify a true consolidation trend and to mark the top and bottom price levels. They should also be able to spot signals indicating potential breakout, and to reveal whether breakout led to a bullish, bearish, or new consolidation trend.

Chapter 11

True or false:

1. F
2. T
3. T

Discussion: The student should be able to identify (a) consolidation, (b) breakout signals, and (c) confirmation in the form of a momentum oscillator. The lack of movement into overbought or oversold is the form of confirmation that should be highlighted.

About the Author

Michael C. Thomsett is author of numerous books on the topics of technical analysis and charting. His published works include books from Wiley, FT Press, Amacom, and Palgrave Macmillan, among others. His best-selling book *Options* (10th edition, DeGruyter) has sold over 300,000 copies and has been in print since 1989.

The author is a frequent speaker at investment trade shows and offers online coaching services. He considers the topic of momentum as one of the most overlooked and least understood in the science of technical analysis. His educational website is https://TheMoneyCraft.com

Index

OTHER TITLES IN OUR FINANCE AND FINANCIAL MANAGEMENT COLLECTION

John A. Doukas, Old Dominion University, Editor

- *Welcome to My Trading Room: Basics to Trading Global Shares, Futures, and Forex, Volume I: Foundation of Trading* by Jacques Magliolo
- *Welcome to My Trading Room: Basics to Trading Global Shares, Futures, and Forex, Volume II: Create Your Own Brokerage* by Jacques Magliolo
- *Welcome to My Trading Room: Basics to Trading Global Shares, Futures, and Forex, Volume III: Advanced Methodologies and Strategies* by Jacques Magliolo
- *Enterprise Risk Management in a Nutshell* by Dennis Cox
- *Hypocrisy of the African Public Finance Management Framework* by Kamudoni Nyasulu
- *Numbers that Matter: Learning What to Measure to Achieve Financial: Success in Your Business* by Evan Bulmer
- *The Art and Science of Financial Modeling* by Anurag Singal

Announcing the Business Expert Press Digital Library

Concise e-books business students need for classroom and research

This book can also be purchased in an e-book collection by your library as

- a one-time purchase,
- that is owned forever,
- allows for simultaneous readers,
- has no restrictions on printing, and
- can be downloaded as PDFs from within the library community.

Our digital library collections are a great solution to beat the rising cost of textbooks. E-books can be loaded into their course management systems or onto students' e-book readers.
The **Business Expert Press** digital libraries are very affordable, with no obligation to buy in future years. For more information, please visit **www.businessexpertpress.com/librarians**. To set up a trial in the United States, please email **sales@businessexpertpress.com**.

www.ingramcontent.com/pod-product-compliance
Lightning Source LLC
Chambersburg PA
CBHW061326220326
41599CB00026B/5060